WON'T YOU JOIN THE DANCE?

ANGELA TILBY

Won't You Join the Dance?

A discovery of the Christian Creeds

First published in Great Britain 1985
SPCK
Holy Trinity Church
Marylebone Road
London NW1 4DU

British Library Cataloguing in Publication Data

Tilby, Angela
    Won't you join the dance: a discovery of
    the Christian creeds.
    1. Creeds
    I. Title
    238 BT990
    ISBN 0–281–04170–9

Typeset by J & L Composition Ltd
Filey, North Yorkshire
Printed in Great Britain by
Whitstable Litho Ltd, Whitstable, Kent

For
James Tilby, Sarah Moore, Jonathan Miller,
Jonathan Moore. And Alexandra.

With thanks to
Rosemary Dawn, who picked up the pieces
and to
Jeannie Stirrup and Jeane Moore
who kindly and patiently
did the typing.

AMOR VINCIT OMNIA

ACKNOWLEDGEMENTS

Thanks are due to the following for permission to quote
from copyright material:

The Nicene Creed and the Apostles' Creed from
The Alternative Service Book 1980 are
© International Consultation on English Texts
and are reproduced with permission.

Extracts from 'Lord of the Dance' and 'Carol of the Creatures'
by Sydney Carter
reprinted by permission of Stainer and Bell Ltd and
Galaxy Music Corporation.

The extract from 'Jesus the Dancing Master is'
reproduced by permission of Holt, Rinehart & Winston Inc.

CONTENTS

INTRODUCTION

Will you won't you will you won't you will you join the dance?
Will you won't you will you won't you won't you join the dance?

From *Alice in Wonderland* by Lewis Carroll

The creeds have had a bad press for many years from Christians and non-Christians alike. They have come to stand for what most people dislike about formal religion.

I have to confess that I have always been secretly fascinated by the *oddness* of the creeds: their solemnity, their baffling refusal to explain themselves, their enigmatic brevity and the enormous amount of useful, relevant and interesting information that they leave out.

This is an attempt to explore the creeds, not as dead dogmas, but as living symbols which reach out to, and reflect back, the mystery of the universe. That mystery is here seen as a DANCE: a long, round, gracious dance with very simple steps, lots of room for improvization, lots of changes within a constant, evolving pattern. This is the dance of creation – of galaxies, atoms and molecules, living cells, minds and bodies, angels and intelligences seen and unseen, the living, the dead and the unborn. The creeds, when we crack them, contain the secret that all this flowing and swirling, changing and stillness originates and unfolds within the love-dance of God, the Trinity.

This is not a history or commentary or a textbook of doctrine. It is meant for those who would like to follow the Christian way (or find that they *are* following it) but are puzzled about the implications of saying:

I believe . . .

1

INVITATION TO THE DANCE

'Dance then, wherever you may be
I am the lord of the dance,' said he,
'And I'll lead you all wherever you may be
And I'll lead you all in the dance,' said he.

SYDNEY CARTER

Creeds

Creeds are not popular.

They represent a number of things which people find objectionable about Christianity, things which are as much of a problem for the average believer as for the unbeliever.

Creeds are suspect because they look, and sound, authoritative. They contain beliefs formalized into words. They come from the past. They are recited together in church Sunday by Sunday.

Put all these things together and you have a recipe for revolt. The creeds have come to epitomize divisive dogmatism, obscurantism and unthinking conformity, the sort of religion that is learnt and recited by rote. Non-churchgoers pick on the creeds as a reason for their dislike of formal religion. Churchgoers grumble about them and distance themselves. The creeds are there and apparently can't be got rid of, but at least they can be ignored, consigned to the dust-heap of the Christian past. It has been remarked that children, brought up in present-day churches, know only one thing about the creeds and that is that they don't matter. The only time they come across the word 'creed' is when they sing in school or church Sydney Carter's song 'When I needed a neighbour,' which ends each verse with the bouncy little chorus: 'And the name and the colour and the creed don't matter . . .' The song almost implies that to accept a creed is to be rather unbalanced and fanatical. 'Creed-ism' could be on the way to becoming a collective sin, like racism, ageism and sexism.

What are the problems with the creeds? There are four main ones, which, when they are looked at closely, are seen to overlap. They are the problem of the creeds as authoritative statements, the problem of putting religious beliefs into words, the problem of giving authority to what appear to be factual statements about the past, and the problem of owning a belief that is communal. These are not problems to be brushed aside lightly. But they do contain certain misunderstandings about what creeds are and how they are meant to function.

When these misunderstandings are sorted out creeds become far less difficult and obscure and worrying. In fact our dislike of them, rather than being a sign of independence and courage, comes to look more like a symptom of evasiveness and cowardice on our part. We are among those who, for dark reasons of our own *'will* not join the dance' to which the Christian gospel invites us, and of which the creeds are the formal choreography.

Authority

We start with the problem of the authority of the creeds. We are passing, at the moment, out of an individualistic age into a more authoritarian one. Religion, however, for most people remains a matter of conscience and individual choice. My view of God and the church is at least as good as yours. Creeds cause a certain amount of offence because, by their very existence, they hint that this might, in fact, not be the case, that there might be authorities higher than both of us.

Christians acknowledge a number of different sources of authority. Some emphasize the Bible, others the tradition of the Church, others the voice of individual conscience. The creeds do not claim to be authorities. They do not begin 'I believe in the creeds . . .' In fact, they read more like lists of *other* authorities: God, Jesus Christ, the Holy Spirit, the Church. Religious people can be rather undiscriminating about authority. Some who baulk at reciting the creeds have a quite naive and childlike faith in the literal truth of the Bible, or of the undeviating correctness of their vicar's point of view or their own.

The creeds, if they are authorities, are rather humble ones. They point elsewhere. They are more like the index to a book than the book itself. What they index for us is the Christian experience. They give us a list of things we shall stumble across if we continue on the Christian pilgrimage. They remind us that Christian faith is broader and deeper than the experience of any one individual. They handle big themes, mostly in short terse words and phrases, as if to warn us against getting bogged

3

down in religious trivia or pious sentimentality. In fact, if we use them properly, the creeds can protect us against various oppressions. They protect us against the oppression of a faith that is too narrow. They protect us from 'charismatic' individuals who consciously or unconsciously want to manipulate us into a dependent immature faith. They protect us from control by mediocre ecclesiastical bureaucrats. They protect us from the oppression of intellectual fashion. They protect us from the pettiness of our own religious prejudices. The creeds are windows on to new possibilities of believing rather than doors closed against the sharp winds of inquiry or doubt.

Words

The creeds possess a certain sharpness and clarity. They are the expression in words of the deepest beliefs of Christianity. For many, this is another problem. Putting religion into words makes it too specific. It is too cold and intellectual for those who look mainly for emotional succour in their religion. People cope with this difficulty in different ways. Some claim that they 'don't understand a word' of the creeds. Others feel that they have to engage in a personal struggle, each time they say a creed in church, to 'remember what it means'; otherwise they feel they are being hypocritical. Others pick on phrases which give them particular difficulties and mentally opt out, feeling rather guilty, consciously withholding commitment and keeping quiet during 'the bits I can't say'.

Underneath these particular problems lies the instinct that the most important human experiences are beyond words. To put religious experiences into words is to run the risk of trivializing and distorting them. But the creeds do not claim to *be* the Christian experience. They are allusions to it and reminders of it rather than the thing itself. The Greek word for 'creed' used during the period of the great church councils in the early Christian centuries comes into English as 'symbol'. A symbol is incomplete; it points beyond itself. On its own it is rather baffling. But its very incompleteness presses us to recognize the reality for which it stands. We use words as symbolic reminders quite often in everyday life. The words themselves may be very ordinary. 'Do you remember Paris?' may be a simple inquiry about the geography of the city. But between two people who, say, fell in love during a weekend visit there the question can release a whole flood of memories. 'Remembering Paris' recalls and makes present a frosty walk along the banks of the Seine, Christmas lights in the Champs Elysée, a shared bottle of new Beaujolais in a cafe in Montmartre. And beyond that the question rekindles the memories of excitement and tenderness which lie at the root of the present relationship. Asking the question, saying the words, makes the past present. The words have acted as symbols.

As we come to explore the creeds we shall see that they are symbols of the Christian experience which link us to Christians of all times and ages, all round the world, and with the unborn Christians of the future.

The past

This leads us on to the next problem which is the problem that the creeds are so very old. They are not, of course, as old as the Bible. But they clearly do belong to the past. Even in modern translations the creeds sound as if they come from a different age.

Many people find this link with the past very difficult. Our society is engaged by what is new, immediate and disposable. Churches have kept up with the times, revising their forms of service and styles of communal worship. We have become used to continual and rapid change. The changes in our life style in the last hundred years have been so far-reaching and dramatic that we can barely make sense of the present, let alone assimilate our history. We know, too, how rapidly beliefs have changed about the nature of the world and human life. We have got used to accepting our view of the world as provisional: open to revision.

In all of this we do feel a restlessness, a search for wisdom and depth, personal wholeness and roots. This restlessness drives some towards the churches. The search for stability is very understandable. But though there are some people who hope to find in the churches a fortress of unchanging beliefs and moral values, more people look for community, emotional succour and spiritual space. There is much more unease and agnosticism in the area of belief. 'Beliefs', as we usually understand them, seem too fragile and short-lived to bear the weight of our search. The creeds seem to require our commitment to ancient beliefs that do not and cannot belong to us. People want to find simpler and more immediate ways of being Christians. They want to be less encumbered with formulas and theology. They want direct experience.

What the creeds mean and don't mean by belief will be the subject of the next chapter. But here I want to point out that there is an unhealthy side to our dismissive attitude to the past which can do us damage.

On the one hand we know that we are shaped by the past. Individuals and communities have roots. The past has produced us. The past has shaped us. And yet there is a great deal of pressure on us to deny and repress the past. Many think their own past has no value, and that they can only be free if they cut themselves off from it. We can see this from our attitude to the elderly. The experience of the elderly is not valued in our society. It is sometimes interesting, amusing or entertaining but it is not *useful* to us. In most old peoples' homes and geriatric homes there is a tendency to treat the elderly as little children – to 'reward' and 'punish' them, to pity their weakness and to patronize them in their struggles for dignity.

Yet this is not the whole story. We suffer from our unease with the past. We are guilty about it. We know, in part at least, that we cannot be whole unless we learn to live with it. One of the things that happens to people who are seeking to understand themselves better through counselling or psychotherapy is the recovery of their memories. After a job goes astray or a marriage breaks up one of the obvious questions is 'Where did I go wrong?', and this starts the individual on an exploration of the past, which may go very deep into buried parts of his personal history. Recognizing the lost and buried past may not solve our problems but it may, at least, help us to come to terms with them.

This is true not only in the life of individuals. Memories give us identity. They tell us who we are. In times of rapid change and dislocation it is hard for human groups to cling on to a sense of their own reality. This is why, in our time, threatened races and small nations are so eager to recover and preserve their history. Without history they can have no hope. If real accounts of the past are not available false ones are invented and read back into the past. So we see the beginning of the dangerous process of false mythmaking. Myths that are made on the basis of distortion become propaganda weapons that have power to perpetuate division and hatred. But the distortion and manipulation of memory only happens when real memory has been eroded. Real memory is creative because it provides the seeds of hope for the future.

The Christian Church, like other human groups, needs to safeguard its memory. The creeds are a kind of index of memory. They guide us into huge and complicated collections of memory, like the Bible, like the liturgies and traditions of the Church. Without them we are adrift. Christianity is a rich and strange faith, easily distorted and misunderstood, over-complicated or over-simplified. Without the creeds we can only respond to the Scriptures and the rest of the tradition with the very limited resources of our present experience. But the present time is always unstable. It doesn't contain enough to root faith in reality. Memory is the beginning of understanding.

Communal faith

The thing which is perhaps most objected to about the creeds is the way in which they are *said*. We do not listen passively to the creeds being read, or reflect on them quietly on our own. They are to be said or sung publicly, communally, all together.

Most people think that religious belief is fundamentally private and personal. It may be interesting to discuss the existence of God or the possibility of life after death, but it is distasteful to share one's private beliefs. There is more to this than just shyness. There is in our culture a curious splitting between our public and our private selves. We are unwilling to reveal in public very much of what is deepest to us. We believe that our private selves are really private. We believe that in our private selves we do have an area of personal autonomy which is free from the influence of the world around us. Religious belief or unbelief is located in the area of the private self. It is one of our defences against being swamped. To 'share' our beliefs, to make them public, makes us more vulnerable than we wish to be, open to criticism, argument and change. There is something about standing in rows and solemnly saying a creed together which makes us feel very uneasy.

But Christianity is a communal faith. The central act of Christian worship has its origins in a shared meal. The central ethic of Christianity is love, directed to our neighbours, whether they are friends or enemies. There is a release in this recognition. For it means that the creeds belong to the whole Church. It does not fall to any one individual to work out and proclaim the entire Christian faith. It is a declaration shared by everybody: bishops, theologians, children, organists, Sunday school teachers, flower arrangers, brass polishers, monks and nuns, hermits, tea-makers, the holy and the guilty and the troublesome, doubters and those who go to church only a few times a year, the superficial and unthinking as well as the sensitive and intellectual.

If we accept this it puts the creeds in rather a different light. They are not like oaths taken before a court. We are not required, as individuals, to put our hands on the Bible and swear that as we recite the creed, we know that we are telling the truth, the whole truth, and nothing but the truth. Creeds are statements of commitment and belonging.

There is much more in the creeds than any one individual can contain. They are not meant to pin down our fragile experience in hard, dry little words, they are meant to open us up into a shared identity. Saying a creed is like assenting to a resolution passed at a conference. We may not agree with every word. But that doesn't matter. It is our agreement as individuals to live and work together through the Christian experience as we have received it. The creeds *index* the experience, they are *symbols* of it and they are *resolutions* to stick with it.

We can recognize these functions more clearly if we look more closely at how the creeds came into existence. There are two in regular use today among the majority of Christians. The first is called the Apostles' Creed. This is not because it was written by the apostles, but because it was felt to be a summary of their teaching.

The Apostles' Creed

The Apostles' Creed is short and terse. It consists of a set of statements of belief without any kind of explanation or expansion. It starts with the words, 'I believe'. It is the nearest of the two creeds to an individual confession of faith. And yet it is by no means a private confession. This creed is said in public at some church services. It is also used at baptism. Baptism is the rite of entry into the Christian Church. Today, baptism is usually such a mild and domesticated ritual that we have lost the force of its dramatic and shocking imagery. Baptism symbolizes death and rebirth. A death by drowning and a rebirth in water. It is a refusal of a way of life that is hopeless and moribund and a commitment to a way of life full of hope and promise.

In the early Church baptism was considered so important that it was preceded by months of teaching and training. Baptism was not automatic, even for those who were attracted to the Christian faith. Some were so worried by the life-changing implications of baptism that they put it off until the point of death. In a sense, of course, this was cheating, but it shows how seriously the rite of commitment was taken.

New Christians were baptized into the Church at the feast of the resurrection on Easter Eve. All the imagery associated with Easter, of new life, light and the reversal of death heightened the drama of what was to take place. And the creed, which the new Christian recited at baptism acted as a code and password to the Christian life. It was a verbal key, a summary of vast experience, not only belonging to the person to be baptized, who was, after all, at the very beginning of the Christian life, but belonging to the whole gathered community, to the Church of the present, future and past.

In baptism the new Christian knew he had joined a great company. The creed was his assurance that the essence of the faith was unchanging. The beliefs that he declared did not belong to him alone. They linked him with his roots: with the preachers and bishops and martyrs and saints of the past; with the first Roman and Greek and Jewish converts to Christianity, who had heard the preaching of the apostles, with the apostles themselves who had witnessed the resurrection of Jesus. The beliefs linked him with the reality of Jesus himself, with the gospel of the kingdom preached to men and women with healing and hope, and, before Jesus, the creed linked him to the faith of Israel, the faith of prophets and priests, kings and patriarchs who had searched for and proclaimed God in the wilderness and the city.

The Nicene Creed

The other creed in common use is called the Nicene Creed. Its name comes from a great theological council held in the town of Nicaea (now in northern Turkey) in AD 325. A version of the creed was issued by this council, though the form we have it in today is rather longer and more explicit.

This creed probably started as a baptismal creed. But it developed into a kind of 'norm' of Christian belief under the pressure of competing interpretations. It reflects an age of deep and passionate religious conflict. The Church was torn apart by two radically different viewpoints on the identity of Jesus Christ, both of which claimed to be in line with Scripture and tradition. The Nicene Creed reflects the Church's attempt to produce a unifying resolution. It was intended to unite different factions and to smooth over painful differences. It also aimed, by producing a fairly sharp 'definition' of who Jesus was, to make clear which ideas and teachings about him fell right outside the limits of Christian faith.

9

Today the Nicene Creed is chiefly used at the celebration of the Eucharist. In its modern version it usually starts with the words 'We believe . . .' not ' I believe . . .'. This emphasizes the fact that the Nicene Creed in particular is a communal declaration, belonging to the whole Church. In fact, the relation between the two creeds confirms this. The Apostles' Creed is used at baptism, when the individual declares his faith on his own in the presence of his fellow Christians. But the Nicene Creed is used by everyone when the church celebrates together. We say 'I believe' at baptism in order to be able to say 'We believe' at the Eucharist.

For those who dislike creeds because they suspect they are divisive it might be worth reflecting that the Nicene Creed is practically the only thing which the churches hold in common. It has often been suggested as a basis for church unity. The Church has split and resplit down the ages on all sorts of trivial and tragic issues. There are huge differences in the ways in which the different churches understand authority, ministry, sacraments, worship and Scripture. There are differences in politics and lifestyle. But when the Church has split it has not usually been about the creeds. The Nicene Creed is actually a unifying force among Christians, bringing together bits of the Church which are divided by space and time.

Conclusion

In conclusion we can see that the creeds are not quite what we think they are. The hard dogmatic statements that we have imagined them to be turn out to have a more modest function. Yet the function they do have is a real one and it is a challenge to a number of our assumptions about religion.

The creeds are an index of Christian faith and experience. This assumes that there is a content to Christian experience. It is not just a matter of feelings. You can't just make it up as you go along. The creeds are a symbol for realities which can't be finally pinned down in words. Yet what they point to are not arbitrary constructs of the human mind. At the end of faith's quest there is a finding and a recognition of what is not us but other. The creeds are not the reality we seek, but if we use them properly we shall discover that they are accurate signposts.

The creeds are resolutions. They are statements of commitment and belonging. We share our faith with others. The heart of Christian faith is not individual believing but a shared quest, a communal pilgrimage, a dance. Our quest is shared with Christians of the past. To understand the faith we need to take that past seriously, not to deny or repress it, but to use it as a creative memory, a springboard to hope. Our pilgrimage is also communal in the present time. We need to look critically at the commonly made distinction between public and private belief. The creeds are a public and communal possession of the Church. They remind us that in Christianity belief is not essentially a private matter.

What is meant by belief, however, remains a problem. Critics of Christianity sometimes assume that Christians are self-deceived in their beliefs, that they owe allegiance to beliefs which are imcompatible with our knowledge of the world and of ourselves. To this problem we now turn.

2

TAKING THE FLOOR

We believe . . .   I believe . . .

❧❧❧

Divine grace is dancing: fain would I pipe for you.
Dance ye all![1]

The creeds *are* rather forbidding at first glance. They look like
lists of things that have to be crossed off one by one if you are to
count as a Christian: 'I believe in God, yes, that's all right . . .,
the Father Almighty, yes, I'll go along with that . . .'

For some, the real problems start further down the list with
things like the virgin birth and the resurrection: 'I'm not at all
sure about *this* . . ., I really can't swallow *that*!' There are those
who go through agonies because there are bits of the creed that
they can't say. They feel hypocritical reciting the creeds in
church and wonder whether they are really Christians at all.

Others find the whole business objectionable. Christianity,
they say, is a practical religion. Jesus didn't teach his disciples
creeds, he taught them to pray and to love one another and to
forgive. The theory behind it, represented in the creeds, is of no
relevance to the ordinary layman. The assertions of the creeds
only confuse simple Christianity. They are, after all, only
human opinions, better left to be dissected by theologians. They
can't be proved or disproved, so why waste time worrying
about them?

The creeds are assertions of *faith*: '*I believe* . . .', '*We believe* . . .'

Faith and facts

Having faith is not the same as having proof or certainty. But
neither is having faith the same as holding an opinion. Faith is
commitment without certainty. This is difficult. It is like walking
a tightrope. Faith is always in danger of becoming something
else. It is always under pressure to weaken itself into 'mere
opinion', or to fortify itself with 'solid reasons' into certainty.

The age we live in puts its own peculiar pressures on faith.

We live in an age of facts. This is our heritage after hundreds of years of science. Science describes the world by experiment and proof. Proof is real information. It is knowledge. Knowledge is power, the means of control over our environment. One of the reasons science has been so successful is that it appears to be wholly objective, untainted by human passion and prejudice. Though many have come to question whether *any* human enterprise can really be that objective, not least scientists themselves, most of us accept the real achievements of the scientific age. With that, we put a high value on facts. A fact, we are taught be believe, is a fact. It is the way the world is, whether we like it or not.

So we live in an age of facts. This is the information age. Information comes to us from all directions. It comes clothed as facts, as 'the truth'. Sometimes information turns out not to be true. It is composed of false facts. It is dis-information. If what comes to us cannot be shown to be either facts or false facts, then it loses value. It becomes 'mere opinion'. The 'opinionated' person is the person who is biased, one-sided, who hasn't got enough respect for facts.

The high value we put on facts means that there is a lot of pressure on believers to demonstrate that their beliefs have a high factual content. Beliefs must stand up for themselves. They must be seen to be based on an authority which is equal to that of science. At the very least most Christians want assurance that it is more reasonable to believe than not to believe.

Roman Catholics and Protestants are usually taught that faith has a rational basis. There *are* sound intellectual grounds for belief. Christian faith can be put into rational statements. The creeds, superficially, look like rational statements. Their language could be mistaken for data, for the language of science. It appears to be dry, objective and unemotional. Christians have sometimes felt it was their job to argue out the beliefs of the creeds, clause by clause, point by point, from a supposedly firm base of intellectual superiority.

Defending the faith

There is nothing new in the attempt to explain faith. Christianity is an infectious religion. It is told and sung and spread to others. What is new is the relentless *intellectual* pressure to stand up to the opposition. Since the rise of science the Christian churches have been on the defensive.

We can see this particularly in the last century. Scientific thinking was such a threat to theology that the churches were driven to invent quite ludicrous dogmas to protect the *status quo*. The Roman Catholic Church's response to the intellectual revolutions of Marx and Freud was the doctrine of Papal Infallibility. The success of Darwin's theory of evolution contributed to the development of biblical fundamentalism among Protestants. In each case Christian doctrines of authority, which have their basis in the freedom of faith, became hardened into intellectual straightjackets. Such doctrines continue to appeal to the insecure, to those who are afraid of freedom, and who want religion to protect them from harsh reality.

Not all reactions to the success of science have been so extreme. Many more moderate Christian thinkers have tried to put themselves into the shoes of the unbeliever and to build up cumulative arguments for the reasonableness of faith. These attempts are often beautifully constructed and rationally argued. But they don't often persuade non-believers to become believers. What they usually succeed in doing is to strengthen the faith of those who are already committed, or who are on the brink of commitment and are, perhaps unconsciously, looking for something to tip them over the edge.

One of this country's most successful evangelists, Canon Michael Green, has written a number of short, attractive paperbacks designed for young, thinking people. They are cogent and persuasive – to those who are newly converted, or who are already half convinced. C. S. Lewis's magnificent *Mere Christianity*, based on a series of radio talks, gave a new confidence to a generation whose faith had been tried by the depression and the war years. John Austin Baker's lucid and passionate account of Christian belief in *The Foolishness of God* helped many to find connections between their faith and the world disclosed by science and history. Hans Küng's huge work *On Being a Christian* helped Catholics and Protestants to recognize what they had in common and where they differed from Marxists, atheists and adherents of other religions.

But to the outsider these attempts to defend and commend Christian faith remain baffling. The arguments, so neat and persuasive to the believer, seem circular and arbitrary to the non-committed. The unbeliever knows instinctively that the roots of faith are not rational. Faith is not, in the end, based on facts. It is a stranger and more mysterious response to reality.

Faith may be buttressed, strengthened, weakened or distorted by reason and argument. But it is never created by reason.

The search for certainty

This is unnerving. It means that Christians have to recognize that for many, in our fact-based society, faith is simply not possible. It also suggests that true faith might be rather subversive. It might undermine in some quite devastating way our conditioned responses to reality.

But that we must leave for the moment. It is true, however, that many people realize that faith is deeply at odds with the world. They feel driven by this dilemma not to question the world but to test the assertions of faith against the conclusions of modern thought. The search is for a bedrock of fact which is strong enough and simple enough to support the weight of commitment.

For over 150 years scholars and critics, theologians and historians have tried to 'get behind' the creeds and Scriptures. They have supposed that by applying the rational procedures of scientific investigation they would emerge with some solid knowledge. Much has been achieved. We have discovered, through their labours, a good deal about how the Scriptures were put together, and the background to the events which faith celebrates.

The real Jesus

One of the longest searches has been the search for the real Jesus. The assumption is that the irrationalities of faith, expressed in creed, dogma and myth, have obscured the historic figure who gave rise to them. Honest scholarship can reveal the real man from Nazareth. The figure to be discovered may well turn out to be very different from the Christ worshipped in churches. In fact, because the Christ of faith is so baffling to reason, it is almost a presupposition that he should turn out to be very different. He *has* to be more accessible than the strange Christ of the creeds.

In recent times the search for the real Jesus has attracted a wide following. Like Rabbit's friends and relations on the Long Search for the North Pole,[2] the procession has been joined by 'investigative' journalists, novelists, playwrights, film-makers, teachers and politicians. All make the assumption that, given honest and rational inquiry the real Jesus will be uncovered. They go at it with pen and camera, tape-recorder and typewriter.

New portraits of Jesus emerge which are attractive and convincing. Some are conservative and reverent in tone, others are excitedly reported as 'shocking' to the faithful. Most seem light-years away from the solemn, dogmatic and repetitious patterns of the creeds. The portraits that emerge, however, are not long-lasting. Often what is most clearly revealed are the investigator's presuppositions, his conscious or unconscious 'needs'. We all have a habit of creating a Jesus-figure in our own image and after our own likeness.

So, the Jesus who was 'discovered' by the liberal theologians of the last century bore a strange resemblance to a nineteenth-century liberal. The Jesus respected by Marxist thinkers is a utopian revolutionary; the Jesus respected by psychiatrists is a figure with a unique understanding of the human dilemma. A Cambridge don finds a witty, ironic Jesus; a Jewish scholar finds a charismatic rabbi; a feminist finds a Jesus unusually liberated for his time in his approach to women. A popular songwriter finds a superstar betrayed by his success; an agonized playwright depicts Jesus struggling with his identity. And so on.

The historian, theologian, journalist or ordinary believer all share the same problem. They have nothing but the original documents to go on. There is no way to Jesus that by-passes the baffling ambiguities of Scripture and tradition. Scripture and tradition arise from faith. There is no independent viewpoint. There are no other memories or reports available.

Faith seeking understanding

Of course it is possible that creeds, tradition and scriptures may have misunderstood Jesus. The whole pattern of believing mapped out in the creeds may be based on a colossal mistake. But we have no final way of knowing. Certainty is not available. If we wish to enter the Christian experience we have no other option but to enter the community of faith and try it out. There is no safe ground from which we can survey the territory of faith from a distance without putting our feet on the road. Faith is experiential and not theoretical. Christian discipline, the life of the creeds, is rather severely practical. Before we can hope to understand we must give our attention. Faith seeks understanding. It is not the other way round. Facts do not bring us to faith, even though many Christians wish they would and think they can. Instead, faith questions our fact-based assumptions and teases us to think new thoughts. 'The questioning involved here is not our interrogation of the data, but its interrogation of us.'[3]

The world of fantasy – the underside of facts

It is not true, of course, that all Christian believers look for facts to base their faith on. There are probably just as many who are quietly convinced that faith has nothing to do with reason or facts at all. Facts and faith operate for them in quite separate spheres. To say 'I belive . . .' is to make a commitment that is primarily personal and emotional.

To understand why this is so, we must recognize that there is an underside to our fact-based view of reality. Modern men and women do not live by data alone. Our fact-based world is hard, neutral, objective and not at all human. That is why we value it. We admire and respect, and fear, computers precisely because they are not swayed by emotion. But the world of facts hurts us. It bruises our minds. That is why we give them 'generous holidays in the world of fantasy'.[4]

We consume, in our fact-based society, massive amounts of fantasy. Much of it comes through television. The video display unit, which disseminates computer facts, also entertains us with video fantasy; fiction, games and other entertainments. We are ambivalent about our fantasies. 'Serious' people, especially those who are successful in the world of facts, virtuously declare that they never have time to watch television. Others admit that they spend evenings 'in front of the box', either with a sense of shame because they should have been doing something more productive, or with the air of those who have enjoyed a well-earned treat.

We are not sustained by the world of facts, however much we feel we ought to be. But we don't think of our fantasies as having much practical value. They are a retreat from reality. Fantasy is the underside of the world of facts.

An age dependent on science produces, almost as a by-product, the industry of science fiction. Some quite famous scientists write science fiction for relaxation, and very odd the results are too. Science excludes what cannot be proved. And so the unprovables return in science fiction. They return in fantastic form as powers of light and darkness, unearthly intelligences, travellers through space and time. It is as though the horror and glory of our inner experience, denied in the world of facts, is projected in science fiction on to the vast canvas of the universe. Outer space is a symbol for the inner space that our fact-based world forbids us to explore.

Therapeutic fantasy

Religion can function in our age of facts as a therapeutic fantasy. Marx described religion as 'the heart of a heartless world'. Freud thought it was a sign of failure to cope with hard reality. The followers of these great and subtle thinkers have assumed that such judgements merely diminish religion and unmask it as an illusion. But the same judgements could be taken to show that there is something lacking in our perception of reality. We need what religion stands for, even if we reject its claims to truth.

Today quite a few sophisticated believers candidly admit that their religious practice goes hand in hand with atheism or agnosticism.[5] Many more demonstrate, without quite admitting it, that they are, in fact, using religion as an emotional prop, and that it has nothing to do with their real judgements about how things are.

So believing can be seen as a mental trick that we play on ourselves. It is a 'trip' from the cold world of facts to an imaginary world of love and purpose. To say a creed then becomes a method of pulling ourselves up by our own boot-straps. We imagine God. 'God' stands for all that we can think of as powerful and good. He is a focus for our hopes and aspirations. Of course we know that he does not really exist. But 'believing' in him helps. Saying prayers, singing hymns or reciting creeds is like whistling in the dark to keep our strength up. It is like hugging a teddy bear when we are afraid or lonely. The teddy bear cannot respond to us. But he is designed to give us comfort. He is furry, solid and dependable. He looks and feels like the comfort that we want for ourselves.

A 'little corner for religion'

If we accept the split between fact and fantasy, if we put a high value on facts and are ambivalent about our fantasies we can make a little corner for religion in our hard, dark world. Those who find religious fantasy helpful will go to church, pray and say creeds. Those who don't will find other sources for kindling their own courage and endurance.

Yet, for most people, this form of 'faith' is bound to seem rather eccentric. It clearly falls short of the intentions of those who wrote the scriptures and hammered out the creeds. Whatever they believed God to be, they believed him to be real, the most real thing there is, not a mere metaphor for human goodness or power. Faith-without-facts is essentially a private and emotional response to reality. But creeds, as we saw in the last chapter, are public, open statements of commitment that link us to the past and future. Faith, in the sense that the creeds require it, is faith in what cannot be proved but is believed to be true by the huge company of believers. Faith-without-facts gives only private and individual meanings to the shared human experiences of good and evil, light and darkness. In the end, it falls short of reality.

The search for a faith based on facts and the search for a faith without facts have more in common than we might have supposed. Both accept the split between fact and fantasy. Both accept that the real world is composed of hard, proven facts, and whatever does not belong to this world must be relegated to the world of fantasy. And both lead to distortions when it comes to particular points of belief. We shall see this more closely by looking at some particular examples.

'Believing in' the resurrection

The resurrection is often described as the corner-stone of Christian faith.

... as a fact

There are Christians who are convinced that the resurrection is 'the best-attested fact in history'. In other words they look to the authority of proven facts to back faith. They produce what they think is evidence and build it into apparently persuasive arguments. One well-loved example of this kind of strategy is Frank Morison's *Who Moved the Stone?*, in which the author sets out to convince his readers that the evidence for the empty tomb is irrefutable.

Some are convinced. But most people aren't. They suspect, rightly, that the wrong kind of arguments are being used. The more watertight the argument appears the more trivial the whole exercise seems to become. There is something missing. What is missing is the dimension of faith.

The resurrection, whatever else it was, is not reported in the New Testament as if it was something that simply 'happened'. The stories about it are too loaded with mystery, with the sense that it represents the breakthrough of something that is outside the range of our normal experience. To familiarize it, to make it ordinary, to make it, in other words, a *mere* fact, is to lose the point. When we look at the arguments of books like *Who Moved the Stone?* we can see that they are not so much invitations to faith as attempts to clobber us into orthodoxy by seemingly rigorous argument. That the argument does not for a moment stand up to critical examination is, of course, another issue.

... as a fantasy

Some have no need of empty tombs. Quite the reverse. They know in their minds and hearts that dead men don't rise. It is impossible that they ever could or would. They want to separate 'faith' from the real world of facts. For them the 'resurrection' is a symbol. It represents an emotional reality in the life of the believer. What is happening here is that religious language is being commandeered to describe everyday experience. And again, most people aren't convinced. They suspect, rightly, that the resurrection of Jesus is not at all necessary to the emotional experience. It adds nothing to it. Any example of goodness triumphing over evil or ideals surviving disaster would do just as well.

The first strategy is manipulative. It seeks to coerce. It takes away from the freedom of faith. The second, though, is vacuous and, in the end, sentimental. But what is basically wrong with both of them is that they involve a dishonest reading of the texts.

The accounts of the resurrection in the Gospels and the Acts of the Apostles form a very untidy set of stories. There are huge inconsistencies between the accounts. The accounts themselves are ironic and inconclusive. The resurrection of Jesus did not sweep away all doubts. It created new ones. Jesus appeared only to his friends who had abandoned him. They had difficulty in recognizing him. They responded to the mysterious event with fear and joy, disbelief and recognition. The accounts seem to leave us with the challenge to believe. But it is not a challenge based on factual evidence. It is a challenge based on our *recognition* of Jesus as the one in whom God has acted to save us.

The arguments which seek to prove the resurrection as a fact among facts ignore this. They seek to make the accounts consistent, which is the last thing they are. Somehow they have misunderstood the nature of the event. It is, in the Gospels, a breakthrough, a revelation. It requires the response of faith.

The sceptic, on the other hand, will read his own dishonesties into the account. He will tend to assume that the supernatural elements can simply be ignored. He will choose to consider the resurrection as a phenomenon to be *explained*. So he will construct a rational explanation that fits his own naturalistic presuppositions. The explanation becomes, inevitably, an explaining away. He removes the real problem by dividing the story up. The supernatural bits go into the world of fantasy. Anything left is retained in the world of facts.

Both strategies remove the real problem and replace it with more congenial ones.

Staying with the story

But simply to read and stay with the resurrection stories is to be baffled. It is to encounter questions and untidied ends. To label it as mere fact or dismissable fantasy is not to do the texts justice. For whatever the resurrection was it took place in the dark, not only of earth's night but of human ignorance. What was perceived took place in the half-light of dawn or sunset. The stories are pointed to only one end. Will we believe or disbelieve? Will we recognize, in Jesus, the suffering and the victory of God?

Faith is not coming to rational conclusions about these stories. It is a kind of suspension of judgement, a deliberate probing, not only with the mind but with the heart and the imagination. In the story, as it comes to us, is the possibility of revelation. Our eyes, too, can be opened to see the risen Lord. The rhythm of the resurrection story can set us *dancing*, bringing into co-ordination our separated minds, hearts and bodies – the mind in fascination and probing, the heart in love – the body in worship and doing and telling.

'Believing in' the virgin birth

The virgin birth is one of the hardest bits of the creeds:

> He was conceived by the Holy Spirit
> and born of the virgin Mary . . .

> By the power of the Holy Spirit
> he became incarnate of the virgin Mary
> and was made man . . .

Did it happen?

Most people assume that the most important issue here is whether or not it actually happened. The issue is usually settled, one way or another, in terms of presuppositions. We either

21

believe it could have happened or that it couldn't have. We either strain to justify its inconclusion in the world of more bizarre and unlikely facts, or else we ditch it, with relief, into the world of fantasy.

It is more of a problem than the resurrection. If the resurrection is relegated to the world of fantasy at least it remains, for Christians, as an *essential* fantasy, very close to basic human and Christian hopes of life springing from death. But the virgin birth, once it is seen as fantasy, ceases to have any function at all. It becomes rather an embarrassment. So what are we to make of it? There is no doubt that, seen as a fact, the virgin birth encounters many objections. It is biologically unlikely, though not entirely impossible.

A fairy tale?

But, more seriously, it doesn't quite *read* as a factual account. The Gospels of Matthew and Luke present it in a religiously imaginative way. It is loaded with particular symbols and prophecies, like a fairy tale. Many scholars suggest that we should see it as a pious invention, linking the arrival of Jesus with certain predictions in the Jewish scriptures and expressing devotion to him as Messiah and Son of God.

But here we encounter a problem. Fairy story it may be, but it is a fairy story that Christian scholars and serious-minded critics *don't like* very much. The resurrection stories can be linked, rightly or wrongly, to all kinds of human experiences of survival against the odds. But the virgin birth, even as a story, outrages some of our assumptions.

First, it is a story of pure grace. There is no object lesson in heroic faith, no victory won or foes defeated. There is only the submission of Mary to God's will. Feminists don't always like that any more than men do. Second, it is deflating to male fantasies of power, sex, blood and inheritance. The Son of God is 'begotten of no human will'. His arrival marks a radical disruption of the usual power structures. And last, it is very simple, very magical, very much a child's story. Everyone can grasp it. It reminds us of our own childhood, and of our persistent vulnerability. There is something about the story that is unashamedly vulgar and popular. Many of us would prefer God to be rather distant and adult. The possibility that he might choose to communicate with us on the level of our childlike selves is rather alarming.

Much to the irritation of rationalist clergy and theologians people won't forget the virgin birth. It is not the committed 'serious' Christians who are haunted by it as much as the uncommitted. It fills the churches at Christmas year after year.

The instinct of faith

Why do people come to church at Christmas? Not to worship a bizarre fact. Is it then just sentimental fantasy? Many would think so. And yet, those who are moved by the story are not moved by human generalizations drawn out of it. It is the particulars repeated every year, the angels, the star, the crib, the visit of the shepherds and the wise men. The story seems to retain the power to put people in touch with something universal, something deep, which defies our neat categories of fact and fantasy. They meet the story with the instinct of faith. They go with it, suspending disbelief, letting the story speak. They are not committed to its being factually true, but they are not necessarily committed to its untruth either.

When the creeds assert the virgin birth it is as part of what it means to have faith 'in' Jesus Christ. They do not commit us to believing that it happened. Nor are we to disbelieve it as a matter of principle. It is all to do with the recognition of who Jesus is and what his significance is for us and for all mankind. Agonizing as it is in our cut-and-dried age of facts we are to go with the story, suspending rational belief and disbelief. Only if we do this can we begin to realize the significance of what is being said to us. We may come to the story fairly convinced that it did or did not happen. But that is not the point. The virgin birth is not an interesting piece of information. It is not a mere fact. It is part of the mystery of salvation. If our certainty about it is a rational factual certainty we shall lose what it has to reveal to us.

We can lose out on the virgin birth in two ways.

Distortions of reason

If we are convinced that it 'happened' we shall treat it primarily as a historical fact. This will lead us to a number of speculations and deductions. We may decide that virginity is the highest and most spiritual state and that normal sexual relations are a poor second-best. We may conclude that God shuns and despises the normal processes of human sexuality and reproduction. We may decide that God is 'male' because he must have 'impregnated' Mary. We may find it impossible to think of Jesus as a normal human being because the virgin birth makes him physically half-God. These are quite rational deductions, which is precisely what is wrong with them. They are irrelevant to what is being claimed by the virgin birth.

What *is* being claimed is the breakthrough of God into human life. It is about a breakthrough at a particular point of time in a particular place which has set in motion a drastic reordering of human nature. It expresses, in terms which the smallest and simplest and thickest can understand, the great Christian paradox of the incarnation.

The religious value of the story lies in its being received as revelation. Yet this is precisely what, in our fact-based culture, we are incapable of doing. If we regard it as fact, in the sense that we have come to understand fact, we shall fall into the distortions of literalism. But if we regard it as fantasy we are bound to ask, why *this* story? We can see that it has problems for us. If it is *only* fantasy it is easy to write it off as irrelevant and childish, along with Father Christmas.

But if we do write it off we are losing more than we realize. The generation of theologians who dismissed it as 'mere myth' were followed by a generation of theologians who wrote off the incarnation in just the same way. The incarnation itself came to be seen as a fantasy expressing the general truth that God is involved always and everywhere with human beings.[6] The bodily contact of God with human flesh and blood expressed in the doctrine of the virgin birth came to seem vulgar and irreligious. Christian faith slowly began to turn itself into a dry system of rationalist monotheism – a suitable and utterly hopeless and dreary religion to fit the age of facts.

Making sense of the virgin birth means suspending both literal belief and unbelief. It also means recognizing that they have much more in common than we usually realize. Both rely too much on the rational. Both accept uncritically the split between fact and fantasy – the exaltation of the brain and the downgrading of our faculties of wonder and imagination. Both rob us of the fulness of Christian faith, its freedom and transforming power.

Faith, doubt and agnosticism

There are many confusions about faith and doubt. Faith is perfectly compatible with doubt, in fact, it needs it. Doubt keeps us open, critical and questioning. Doubt prevents us from giving false authority to any formula, interpretation or ideology that would stand between us and the object of faith. Sometimes people feel guilty about having religious doubts. But the opposite and enemy of faith is not doubt but un-faith, unbelief. Unbelief springs from a closed mind, a mind that cannot conceive miracle or surprise or true hope. Faith is uncertain, but keeps going. Faith has a lot to do with faithfulness or steadfastness.

The agnosticism, the 'not-knowing' that goes with faith clouds the object of faith from our distortions. Faith involves the endurance of this agnosticism, not its denial. As the mystics of faith know, the cloud of unknowing is only pierced by love.

The distortion of faith

Our concept of faith is distorted. The distortion has a long history. In the history of the Western Catholic church it goes back at least to the Middle Ages and it was inherited by the churches of the reformation. The problem is that we have confused the mystical knowledge that faith gives with other forms of knowing.

Take the idea of God. The idea of a supreme being has always been important in human thinking. It is a useful and plausible way of explaining the world and ourselves. In medieval Christian Europe the idea of God underpinned the whole structure of human knowledge. Without the notion of a supreme being the world was incomprehensible. Faith and reason went hand in hand, and the church blessed them both. Belief came to be seen as the rational acknowledgement of an obvious fact.

What was lost in this alliance of faith and reason was the essential character of biblical and credal faith. Faith is commitment to what is beyond all other forms of knowing. It is a free act, an act of exploration. It can never be the same thing as an acknowledgement of the obvious.

The Catholic and Protestant churches, on the whole, misunderstood this. They allowed their mystics and saints to speak of the dark night of faith, but mysticism, the life of prayer, was separated from theoretical theology. This is why the success of science proved such a threat. Science explained the world without God. The rational structure of faith was under attack. But what science was actually eroding was false faith. From the standpoint of real faith the God who is part of our mental furniture cannot be God. He is an idol. The God who undergirds a rational picture of the universe is only a concept in our minds. What faith seeks cannot be proved or disproved by argument. That which faith seeks must be bigger than all our thoughts about him.

What faith seeks is too big to be perceived by man's reason, and also so small and elusive that it is bound to be overlooked. The 'other' that faith seeks can only be known if he discloses himself. And he discloses himself not to the rational mind which will reduce him to a mere fact among facts, and not to the restless emotions which will merely project on to him their own frustrations and needs. His discloses himself to *faith* which alone is empty enough and open enough to perceive him.

It is through faith that both the rational mind and the emotions are brought together. Both are recreated in the dialogue of faith with the 'other' that it seeks. Faith is daring to step into a dance that is already going on. It is the dance of creation with its God. We recognize, dimly, the rhythm, but we do not yet know the steps.

So faith is commitment. Not to a supreme being who we invent to answer our questions and comfort our hearts, but to the reality that has invented us. That is why faith is subversive.

Faith cannot accept the removal from reality of all that is not provable fact. It rejects the downgrading of the unprovable into fantasy. Faith also sees that the split we have created has damaged us. It has given us the illusion that we control things. As human beings we do not dictate reality. We are part of it, products of it, like stars and worms, stones and flowers. We are part of the moving dust of the universe but, unlike the dust, we dream. The power of dreaming is something we have received from reality. It attunes us to its rhythms. From dreaming comes our reason, our imagination, our curiosity and inventiveness. Also our loneliness, our need for love, our courage and our terror.

The split in our perception of reality can be described in different ways. It can be seen as a split between the head and the heart, between the brain and the rest of the body, between reason and emotion. The heart, the body and the emotions are our roots in reality and in the fact of our dependence. Splitting them off has given us the illusion of god-like power. It is as though we have left the dance of creation and gone to our corners, angry, sulking, shy and separate. All this is familiar.

We know that we have come to the edge of catastrophe. We know that the planet, and the human race, are in danger of destruction.

Any recognition that there is something wrong with us is a small act of protest. Implicit in this protest are the seeds of faith. This is disquiet with the present and a longing for a deeper, truer reality than the present has to offer. Often it is those who have lived their lives most deeply in the world of facts who recognize most clearly the dangers that we are in. They point us to the recovery, or discovery of *faith*. The proof of human faith in this dangerous age is not in the computer or in the test tube, but in what a Christian poet has called 'the laboratories of the spirit'.[7]

The sense that there is something which is not 'us' but 'other' is fairly universal. It teases and torments men and women of all times and places. It persists, and even flourishes under political regimes which are committed to rubbing it out. 'God' cannot be erased from the human memory. The awareness of God, the regret for God's absence, the hope for God's return seem to be ineradicable.

We cannot know that the 'other', that 'God', is not an illusion. The sense of God could be a sad trick of human consciousness centuries adrift in a lonely universe. We cannot know with certainty which religious or philosophical interpretation of the 'other', if any, comes closest to the truth.

But if we are pressed, by guilt or compassion, loneliness or curiosity, to explore this mystery more deeply we need sign-posts. We need to take on a specific tradition of wisdom. To stay on our own doing a bit here and a bit there is to treat the search for faith merely as an interesting hobby. It is to stay in the shallow end. To go deep we need instruction.

In the creeds we encounter the Christian interpretation of the 'other', of 'God'. He is identified as the source of all that is. A tiny and unique human focus is found in the life and death of Jesus of Nazareth. On the basis of the memory of Jesus the creeds assert that God is not abstract or solitary, but personal and communal, a relationship of eternal love reaching out to embrace and fulfil all created things.

Christianity is a happy and hopeful faith. It shares a good deal with the other faiths in the world, and with those who are motivated to a kind of humanistic faith through concern for our future. It amplifies other faiths in some respects, and is amplified by them in others. In entering deeply into Christian experience through the creeds we shall find that we are not cut off from people of other faiths, but that our links with them are made stronger. In making our affirmations we enter into theirs, as they, making theirs, enter into ours.

Meanwhile we endure the agnosticism which comes from having faith in a rational, critical age. This agnosticism must be our ally, not our enemy, encouraging us to watch out for false authorities while sticking faithfully to a precise form of love and prayer, struggle and suffering. This 'living out' is what is meant by 'believing in'. The real enemy is not suffering or doubt or even the distortions of human longing which faith calls sin. It is depression, hopelessness. Faith lives, with doubt and hope, in a universe of possibilities.

NOTES

1 From the score of *The Hymn of Jesus* by Gustav Holst, which is his own translation of part of the apocryphal Acts of St John.
2 See A. A. Milne's *Winnie-the-Pooh*.
3 Rowan Williams, *The Wound of Knowledge* (Darton, Longman & Todd 1979), p. 1.
4 I am particularly indebted in this chapter to the argument of Peter Brooks, *Communicating Conviction* (Epworth 1983), especially pp. 17–18.
5 The most rigorous exponent of this point of view is the Anglican theologian Don Cupitt. See especially his *Taking Leave of God*, (SCM Press 1980).
6 John Hick (ed.), *The Myth of God Incarnate* (SCM Press 1977), especially chapter 9.
7 R. S. Thomas, *Laboratories of the Spirit*, (Macmillan 1975).

3

WHO CALLS THE TUNE?

[We believe] in one God,
the Father, the almighty,
maker of heaven and earth,
    of all that is,
seen and unseen.

[I believe] in God,
the Father almighty,
creator of heaven and earth,

∞∞∞∞

I danced in the morning when the world was begun
And I dance in the moon and the stars and the sun . . .

SYDNEY CARTER

If faith is a free act in a universe of possibilities, who is the 'object' of faith, the one whom, as the greatest of medieval theologians, St Thomas Aquinas, claimed, 'all men know as "God"'? The question is not simple. We use the word 'God' in two quite different ways. We rarely recognize this because the two uses overlap.

The first use is to speak of God as a theoretical possibility. 'God' is a supreme being who might or might not happen to exist. The question of God's possible existence interests, even fascinates, many people. Philosophers, scientists and theologians wheel out their arguments point by point, for or against. It's all rather like a game and we enjoy it because we enjoy the demonstration of the cool skills of argument and debate.

The question of the existence of God, 'Does God exist?', expects the answer 'Yes', 'No', or 'I don't know'. It is a cool question which expects to be discussed on the basis of evidence and argument. Believers get lured into the debate in good faith. They join in hoping to provide information in favour of the existence of God.

The problem is that the debate *cannot* come to a real conclusion on the basis of facts and evidence. The debate turns out to be a mock debate – a game. The evidence of believers, the

29

information that they so willingly and trustingly confide, simply does not count in the world of facts. They are driven back, usually, to recounting their personal experiences, or to speaking uneasily about 'faith' or 'mystery'. But by then it is too late. The game is lost. The unanswerability of the question leaves the unbelievers smugly certain. Because the believers have failed to produce evidence in terms of the game's question, God *cannot* exist. There is no room for him in the hard, narrow world of facts. If he has a place at all it can only be in the confines of the imagination of the individual believer.

The game of whether or not there is a God continues to be popular. Quite recently a theoretical physicist has written a book looking at the issue in the light of new developments in various branches of science.[1] It is all interesting, thought-provoking stuff. The author is not unsympathetic to religion. He believes he is doing a useful job for religious people as well as for scientists. His aim is to close off what he regards as untenable options for belief, while opening up the rational possibilities that remain. He tells us what kind of a God it is still possible to believe in and what kind of a God must now be regarded as impossible.

Fascinating as this is it is not quite as fascinating, or perhaps as important, as the author would like us to believe. The 'God' he seeks to discover is still a concept in the human mind, a sophisticated and artfully constructed concept, admittedly, but an invented concept all the same, a piece of mental furniture. But the God who is 'allowed' to exist by the grace of science is not, and cannot be, the God of faith, of the scriptures and the creeds.

In the faith of the creeds God is not one whom we hold in existence by thinking him, but the one who holds us. We cannot see him, precisely because he sees the whole of us including the part that sees. There is no 'outside' of his existence from where we can observe him existing. That is why in the end arguments for or against the existence of God have a weary sense of irrelevance. The games are quite fun and even fascinating for intellectually precocious children, but they are not taken all that seriously by grown-ups.

We can see this by the style in which the game is often played. The unbelievers, usually sceptical academics, are on the attack, provocative and mischievous. The believers quickly become evasive. The initial cool question, 'Is there a God' elicits from the more sophisticated believers what appears to be nervous hesitation, 'It all depends what you mean by "God"', or qualification, 'Yes, but not an old man sitting on the clouds'. These evasions and qualifications are interpreted as symptoms of insecurity by the unbelievers. But in fact they are symptoms of a real and well-founded unease with the whole game.

What kind of a God is it that can be so coolly debated? Sometimes a believer breaks all the rules of the game by refusing to respond coolly. Often to the embarrassment of fellow-believers he will bring the questions to an abrupt end by asserting that he has proof that God exists because he spoke to him this morning, or he embarks on a long story of his conversion. Other believers curl up – this is bad form. The unbelievers exchange smiles. This is the genuine article, the real religious nut-case. They close in for the kill. The believer, not realizing his vulnerability goes on bravely and misguidedly, witnessing to the hope in his heart. He loses the game without ever knowing it, and thanks his opponents gallantly for letting him put his point of view.

Sometimes, however, something different happens. The argument moves on to issues of evil, suffering or injustice. Suddenly the tone of the debate alters. There is a rise in temperature. The atmosphere becomes loaded and emotional. Both sides stop talking about God as a theoretical possibility and start communicating in terms of sharp human experience.

The word 'God' now acquires different shades of meaning. The ex-prisoner of war shakes his head and declares he has been unable to believe in God since his terrible experience at the hands of the Japanese. The mother of a small baby is unable *not* to believe in God when she cradles her sleeping child in her arms.

At this point, at the point of losing coolness, the word 'God' begins to be used in a quite different way. It becomes a powerful, deep word, a word that sparks off a shower of strong reactions. Embarrassment, anger, awe, nostalgia, assurance, dread, bitterness, hope, shame, revulsion, bewilderment, wonder – even the hasty withdrawal from engagement into neutral indifference – the word 'God' can arouse all these responses. It is a magic and a potent word, the more so because of our attempts to deny it and rob it of meaning.

I remember when I was quite young having an argument about the existence of God in the playground at school. One of the other girls in my class overheard us. Her best friend was taking part. She led her away quickly from the group of us saying, 'Don't get *involved*! Don't get *involved*!' It seemed such an adult thing to say, and yet it betrayed, not the wisdom of adults, but their fear and caution, their terror of involvement with what cannot be controlled and manipulated by reason or commonsense.

'God' seems to have something to do with trust and betrayal. At a level quite different to that of the cool question, belief or non-belief in God seems to be bound up with our whole experience of reality. Are we held and sustained by reality, brought forth from it and by it and, in some mysterious sense, for it? Or are we finally cheated and deceived by reality, let down, un-encompassed, unsustained?

This is a different way of posing the question of God. It is a way which turns the question on us. We realize, as we ask it, that science and philosophy cannot answer it for us. The answer can only be forged, painfully and personally, as we enter more and more deeply into the question.

To enter the question is a form of faith. It means involvement and commitment to reality. To refuse to enter the question, or to see that there is one, is un-faith, unbelief. Unbelief is easy. It affects us most of the time. The over-reliance on the rational, with which our age is infected and which has led to our present crisis, stems from unbelief and bears fruit in catastrophe. We have tried to control reality and have not seen the question that it asks of us.

The question is a real question, not an answer. What we encounter in the question is God and not God, God present and absent, the reality with which we have to do. We meet the question in unstable situations, when things explode all around us. We meet it at the boundaries of things, on the dangerous edges between life and death, and between death and new life. This is recognized in everyday speech.

'God!' is often used as an explosive word, along with 'Christ!' or 'Jesus!' The word signifies a rise in temperature, an engagement, usually a conflict with reality. It is an oath, apparently a blasphemy. It is interesting that the pious rarely use the name of God explosively. It is almost as if they want to protect God from the place where the non-pious know instinctively he is to be found, that is in the collisions, disruptions, calamities and catastrophes of life.

32

In such dangerous places the word 'God' has meaning not only as an explosion, but as a name. In grief or anger or threat people who don't pray beseech God. It doesn't matter, at such times, whether they believe in God in the theoretical sense. God is the name for what they encounter. A presence and also a heart-rending absence. He is luminous and all-encompassing. He is also dark, empty and silent.

Conventional religion and, for that matter, conventional unbelief do not always allow for the ambiguity of our experience. Conventional religion and unbelief offer answers, not questions. Answers can be taken or left. But questions probe and tease and torment and transform. Often people go through the forms of conventional religion, or conventional unbelief, because of a desire to keep reality at bay. For the conventionally religious person God has his place, his little corner. But the enterprise of faith in God is not to find a place for him in our lives, but to find our place, as it were, in the much vaster and more alarming reality of his life. Often this is a matter of time and degree. Many people move, perhaps very slowly, from a religious faith which is basically a protective device against pain and disturbance, to a faith in which they are *turned round* to face, engage with, suffer and be transformed by the very pain of existence which they have spent their lives fleeing.

The testing place for faith in God is tragedy. This should not surprise Christians since their whole pattern of faith springs from a crucified victim. Tragedy is the place where conventional belief, and unbelief, is put on trial and exposed.

Imagine two women living on the same estate in a small town. Neither have any formal religious allegiance. Neither appear in church except for weddings and funerals. Both have quite a strong sense of God. Often they think they will live on after death. Their ideas about God are formed from all sorts of bits and pieces, hymns on television during the ironing, a child's Bible, a horoscope that comes true. They don't talk about religion, and they feel uncomfortable in church. If asked, they would describe themselves by the Christian denomination last heard of by their parents' generation because they know they are not anything else.

Then both are hit by disaster. One loses her husband in a car crash. The other is told by her doctor that she has cancer and will probably be dead in a few months. Both are shocked and frightened and grief-stricken. One continues to find a bleak comfort in God who is still with her as a deep sustaining power, helping her through the long nights and days. The other is so hurt and betrayed that she realizes quite coldly that there cannot possibly be a God. The universe is indifferent to her and her pain.

Or another example. In the Nazi death camps many Jewish people who had been faithful to their religion all their lives found themselves up against an evil which shattered their faith forever. There couldn't be a God who could deliver his people to such monstrous destruction. Others discovered in their sufferings a new and darker revelation of God, and worshipped. God was not outside the suffering but inside it, suffering silently with his people out of some unimaginable, unspeakable, necessity.

Tragedy forces us to engage with, or to deny, reality. If we engage, we will find that we are stripped of illusion, humbled and transformed. If we deny we will end up less than ourselves, suspended in a limbo of our defences against truth.

Having faith means looking at the darkness of existence with clear eyes and without despair. Even the housewife who rejected God, or the Jews who gave up their religion after the experience of Auschwitz and Dachau are displaying a kind of faith. From their rejection comes anger and energy. They protest against reality, which is not at all the same thing as denying it, and out of this protest comes a passion for change. Faith of this kind may be a bitter and hurt faith, a faith that wounds. It may harden to the point where forgiveness and compassion become impossible. But it is still closer to the faith of the creeds than the un-faith which refuses to engage, which denies the reality of this world and will only consider God as a question for the detached reasoning mind.

Christianity has at its centre the disturbing image of a man deserted by God – a good man unjustly and cruelly punished by God's holy people outside the walls of God's holy city. Yet the Christian proclamation is good news, 'gospel'. So faith in God is not something which can be broken by the fact of suffering. It is something which is built on the truth of it.

Belief in God means coming home to reality and finding our place within it. Each one of us is a unique interface between the inner world of personal consciousness and the world as it is apart from our experience of it. But what do we mean by 'the world as it is'? By 'reality'? Some people deny that we can speak in this way at all. 'Reality', they say, is merely a word for the arbitrary constructions we put upon our experience. I do not share this view. I do accept, however, that our *perspectives* on reality are very deeply coloured by our expectations of it. Also that these expectations are the fruit of past experiences, and that they have a certain power to determine the way in which we continue to see things. At the same time we recognize that all these expectations are, to a greater or lesser extent, distortions. To recognize that they are distortions is to suggest that there is a reality of which we can speak apart from our distortions of it. This reality may not be directly available to us, but if we did not accept the possibility of it we would be unable to ever modify, correct or change our point of view. I am using the word 'reality' in a practical and common-sense way. The real world does go on, even if 'we' are unborn, asleep or dead. We may not experience its reality in these states, but that doesn't mean that it ceases to be real. (It is *us* whose reality has become questionable.) Belief in God involves a willingness to be exposed to the truth of what is, at whatever risk or cost.

If we are dealing with a God who knows us before we know him, who creates us before we are able to invent him, then what we know of him must come from his own disclosure. This disclosure is not in the first instance to reason, or to the senses, or to the imagination. These are the capacities, as we have seen, with which we invent our gods: the supreme being of the mind and the other false divinities we confect to satisfy our needs and hungers.

The creeds claim that God has disclosed himself in human history and experience. He has spoken his name, and continues to speak it, to men and women. In the name that is disclosed is his nature. But this disclosure of God is not to our normal capacities of recognition. It is, in the first instance, as we have seen, a disclosure that comes when the temperature rises in human affairs. It is a disclosure to our emptiness, to the space in us which cannot be filled by the material world, by the inventions of the mind or the fantasies of the imagination. Into this human emptiness the name of God is spoken and given. And what responds to the disclosure of God's name is faith. Faith is not a capacity which some lucky people possess, as others imagine when they say, 'I wish I had your faith'. Faith is something which is created by and out of the disclosure of God.

After faith, of course, come the processes of thinking about

God and feeling for the reality of God. In more technical language, theology and prayer. But these are not independent activities. We may engage in them without faith, but then they are simply dry and fruitless exercises. In their proper place they are responses to faith and tools of faith. But faith itself remains primary. It is critical and questioning. It cannot rest in the security of the mind's reasons, or be swayed by the realization of the mind's limits. It cannot rest in the warmth of the emotions or be deterred by bleakness or depression. Faith is a way of knowing by un-knowing. It requires the constant ditching of unnecessary intellectual or emotional baggage.

The object of faith, God, is elusive, and all who seek him need to travel light. Because of this the journey of faith has sometimes been likened to a search in the dark, a pilgrimage across a wilderness, a night sea passage. It doesn't always feel as though our painful strivings are contained within the 'dance' of creation. Indeed we may *feel* lonely, alienated and cut off from reality.

To have faith in God means that when we engage with reality, when we celebrate it, question it or suffer under it, we are at the same time being spoken to. We are exposed not to a void or a vacuum or a nothing, but to one who speaks. The creeds summarize the speech of God. Behind them is God's disclosure of himself in a small chunk of human history. We cannot prove or disprove his disclosure in this history any more than we can in our own.

To explore the creeds means to burrow away at their assertions, seeking for ourselves the living and true God who is disclosed and hidden in them. This search for truth, and the willingness to be judged and changed by the reality which we seek, is the background to what the creeds have to say about the nature of God. And that is that he is to be known first as the Father Almighty and as the maker of heaven and earth and everything else that happens to comprise the reality of this strange universe.

God as 'Father' – the problems

There are a number of problems with the idea of God as father. To some it is simply a contradiction of experience. The world is too rough and violent a place to be the creation of a God who wants to be known as 'Father'. To others the word 'father' suggests oppression. To call God 'Father' suggests an unacceptable degree of divine control and a corresponding emphasis on human immaturity and dependence. They think that those who choose to have God as their heavenly father are those who are at the same time making a choice never to grow up. Others, especially women, object to God being thought of in male terms. They assume that because God is known as 'Father' that fatherhood is all that there is to be known of him.

It must also be said that Christian teaching has often reinforced these objections. There are Christians who have denied the roughness and harshness of the world in the interests of a soft and reassuring faith. There are also Christians who have kept others in appalling states of immaturity and dependence, and have backed their actions with appeals to the fatherly authority of God. It is also true that Christianity has probably contributed rather more to the diminishment of women under male authority than it has to their freedom and fulfilment.

God as 'Father' – the Bible

The Christian understanding of God as Father comes from the Bible. In Christian faith the Bible is the human record of God's disclosure of himself. It contains what God has said and is saying to men and women. It also chronicles, often with grim candour, the history of human failure and betrayal in response.

'Father' is used in the Bible as a word of power and tenderness. In the Old Testament it is the people of Israel who experience God as father. He is the one who brings Israel into being. From a disparate group of exiles they have become a nation with a history and a future. The word 'father' for God could be grouped with others, such as 'shepherd' or 'king', which imply a relationship of protective leadership.

From the beginning we see something very significant about the fatherhood of God. He does not choose an established or successful people to adopt. He deliberately adopts the human dregs, a bunch of slaves without pride or past. This adopted people is God's delight. Like a human father he takes pride in his child. He has great hopes and ambitions for Israel. Through this child, Israel, he intends to bring all the peoples of the earth into the orbit of his blessing. So he protects the people of Israel, nurtures them, teaches them, disciplines and punishes them.

Like a human father God gets cross and impatient with his child. He has rages, he withdraws hurt and sulking, he shows his exasperation. Again and again the wayward child, Israel, lets him down. But God can't give up. Even when the people of Israel prove continually that they are incapable of returning his love, God finds himself unable to reject them. His commitment has gone too deep. He turns from his sorrow and anger and tries again.

The Old Testament tells a very human story. It does not hedge it about with warnings not to take the fatherhood of God too literally, or to remember that any human speech about God is inadequate. Quite the reverse. If God is speaking to Israel, and to us, through Israel's history, then it appears that what he wants to say must be said directly, without frills. To understand the speech of God we have to hear it first as we would hear human speech. We must accept the anger and passion and jealousy of the character of God in the Old Testament. Here, the God beyond knowing is speaking to us in a language we know all too well, the language of provocation and conflict, love and betrayal. Even the excessive wrath, the favouritism and the capriciousness of the character of God are part of the way in which he communicates with us.

In our superficially rational, but actually deeply frightened age, we have become so detached from the reality of our own nature that we are quite bothered by the God of the Old Testament. The speech of God is so direct and near the bone that it offends our sense of propriety. We take refuge in the misguided belief that the writers of the Old Testament were primitive and savage, and that Jesus made a lot of 'improvements' to the harsh teachings of the law, the prophets and the writings.

The writers of the Old Testament were sophisticated theologians, teachers and historians. They may sometimes have worked with very early legends and ancient sagas. But they were not naive about God. What they insisted was that God was all the time addressing his people. In the politics and conflicts and intrigues of national and personal life God the father is speaking. We hear him, if we listen, through what happens. We are not the only characters in our life's drama. Recognized or not, acknowledged or not, God is on stage all the time, endlessly engaging with us.

This is what the Old Testament is about. It is as dangerous and vulgar as it would be to portray God as a leading character in a highly dramatic soap opera such as 'Dallas'. What frightens people about this kind of God is that he is a God who *reacts*. He is not a safe God, hermetically sealed in heavenly bliss from the mess of earthly reality. His faithfulness to his adopted child involves human beings in violence and provocation.

The writers of the Old Testament were not naive about God. Alongside the conflicts and the dramas, the dangerous portrayal of God in human terms as father to Israel, goes another language about God. This is the language of poetry and liturgy and wisdom.

The priests and sages of Israel knew that God the Father was not all there was of God. In the book of Genesis they describe the creation of human beings. God makes man 'in his own image, in the image of God he created him; male and female he created them'. The human totality, man, is divided into male and female. Together male and female reflect what exists in God as wholeness and completion. There is not much about the 'motherhood' of God in the Old Testament, and what there is is not very well developed. But there are a few hints of it.

At the beginning of the book of Genesis the Spirit of God is described as 'brooding' over the great deep as one who is 'pregnant' with creation. In a daring and rather unexpected image the prophet Isaiah likens God to a woman in labour struggling to give birth.

Behind and beyond all the speech of God in the Old Testament lies the experience of mystery and darkness. God overwhelms man. He cannot be seen or known in himself. He is surrounded by cloud and storm. He is holy, utterly other and apart from man. His thoughts are not human thoughts and his ways are not human ways.

Against this background the fatherhood of God becomes a disclosure of God's intention. Strange and other though he is, he wills to be known, to be close, to be our friend.

Jesus and God 'the Father'

Jesus had a very clear, direct and personal sense of God as father. He also had a sharp conviction that the special relationship between God and Israel had been abused. The continual turning of God to his people in fatherly compassion, one of the great themes of Judaism, had led, not to his people's repentance, but to pride and self-satisfaction. Jesus thought that his contemporaries had come to the point where they took God for granted. But time was running out for them. While they were sitting back and resting on their laurels God was provoking a huge crisis, which was destined to tear the safe world apart.

In his teaching Jesus went back to the roots. There was nothing special about Israel. God had adopted Israel as his child because she was poor and outcast. Jesus insisted that God the Father continued to adopt the world's victims and rejects. Those who were secure and confident in their own goodness had no need of God's fatherly care.

The trust that Jesus had in God was put to the test in the course of his own life. He taught the poor and the sick to trust in God. But the cost of his ministry was his own rejection. He became the problem, the outcast and eventually the victim of society. His proclamation of God as Father led him through the extremes of temptation, vulnerability, loneliness and betrayal.

Though the evidence is that Jesus' trust wavered in Gethsemane and on the cross he could not abandon his commitment to God. He received the bitterest blows as somehow 'given' by the Father. The trust of Jesus, as he approached the cross, was like the trust of a child who does not and cannot know the full story. The New Testament writers use a word for him which is variously translated as 'child', 'son' or 'servant'. It is as though God the Father, who *does* see the whole story, has to let his child go into great pain and loss for a purpose which he cannot fully explain and from which he cannot protect him. By going through with it, in agony and faith, Jesus enables the Father to work the miracle of resurrection.

The resurrection is the heart of the New Testament and the cornerstone of Christian faith. 'Jesus, raised by the Father' is the Christian gospel. The victim returns alive to those who betrayed and abandoned him. He is preached as salvation to those who judged and condemned him. The return and the preaching are not for the purpose of vengeance: they are to bring good news, mercy and hope to oppressed and oppressors alike. The raising of Jesus vindicates God as Father of the outcast and abandoned. He is also ready to receive and release the oppressors and judges. But first they must recognize the darkness within themselves. They must know their crimes for what they are, and face the fears and disappointments which caused them. Forgiveness and renewal are possible. All who turn in trust to God now share in the sonship of Jesus. When the creeds proclaim God as Father it is this biblical background that they have in mind.

We can see that there is no denial of the roughness and violence of this world. God is Father, in the first instance, of this world's victims. Nor is there a mandate for oppression. Again,

God the Father is closer to those who are under authority than to those who wield it over others. God the Father sometimes provokes division, conflict and rebellion. He is not a safe God.

Nor is there, in the fatherhood of God, a denial or repression of human maturity. God's children are not protected from the need to make decisions and choices. Nor is there any divine guarantee that they will not make mistakes, have accidents and fail. They are expected to grow up. Their growing-up is to be whole and free because of the deep roots they have in assurance. They are not finally constrained by the limitations and excesses of human parenting.

Looking at the story of Jesus it is impossible to maintain the view that trust in God as Father is a symptom of human immaturity. There is a paradox about the obedience of Jesus. Obedience is the most dangerous of the virtues because it can so easily become an excuse for irresponsibility. The obedience of Jesus to the Father was both hard and joyful, both a discipline and a liberation. Jesus seems to have been able, in the very giving up of his own will, to have achieved his deepest desire for the kingdom of God. Renouncing himself, he also impresses us as someone who from beginning to end was wholly and absolutely himself. He was undiminished by fear or fantasy.

In the New Testament we begin to get strong hints that the relationship of Jesus and the Father encompasses more than the earthly life of Jesus. It is a manifestation of a relationship that already exists, Father and Son, within the being of God.

The universal Father

A common distortion of the fatherhood of God arises when it is removed from its biblical context. The Old Testament, as we have seen, has a rather shockingly un-idealized picture of God as father to Israel. It combines this with a sense that the being of God is mystery and hiddenness and otherness, beyond human knowing. God's adoption of the world's victims and outcasts then becomes a real disclosure, a surprise, good news, 'gospel'.

But there is always a tendency to rationalize and idealize God, to invent him for ourselves. God, in human thinking, easily becomes an idealized father. He takes on the strong male characteristics most admired by the society which has invented him. At one time he will be seen as a monarch, at another time as a great law-giver, at another time as a great architect, engineer, scientist or poet. In our time he is a mixture of a liberal democrat and a psychiatric social worker who exudes a general, and perhaps not wholly appropriate, air of benevolence over the planet.

Fatherhood, in one of its forms, then becomes a description of the whole of God. He is the Father. We are his children. This is so near the truth of the Christian gospel that it may be hard at first to see why it is a distortion. Many Christians would be perfectly happy to sum up the gospel in a phrase like 'the fatherhood of God and the brotherhood of man'.

The problem is that such a one-sided view of God flies in the face of human reality, of tragedy, of what, in the Bible, is represented by the cross. Part of the gospel is that there is more to God than God the Father, and what this 'more' is is spelt out in the rest of the creeds. But first we must find out why we need more than an idealized monarchical God.

God Almighty

'God Almighty!' is a phrase to swear with. 'Almighty God', is a phrase which begins a great number of prayers. At first glance the notion of God as almighty is deeply reassuring. It is comforting to think that someone is in control of this strange universe. Yet our day-to-day experience does little to support the notion. We may make our prayers to 'Almighty God', but we continually share people's shock ('God Almighty!') at the disordered state of things.

The religion which proclaims the 'almightiness' of God most vehemently is Islam. According to the Koran the whole universe is in a state of submission to the will of God. Everything that happens is part of his intention. Even the unruly heart of man is subject to his control. It is not surprising that, to outsiders, Islam sometimes seems rather fatalistic.

Christians and Jews describe God as 'almighty'. Yet they don't usually understand 'almighty' in quite such definite terms. Where they do, we see the same sense of fatalism and resignation to the will of God which we find in Islam. This fatalism and resignation is profoundly irritating to those who reject religion. They point out, rightly, that if *everything* is accepted as God's will there is no point in trying to alleviate suffering or move society to care more for its weaker members.

In Christianity and Judaism the word 'almighty' arises in the context of worship. God is worshipped as the lord of hosts, the commander of all the powers of heaven. These powers are the 'seen' and 'unseen' forces of the universe. They include elemental powers and angelic armies. The picture conjured up is of a warrior God leading his troops into battle. Yahweh, the Lord of Hosts, rides on the winds and clouds, wades through the waters, drives a fire chariot. The angels of his purpose range between earth and heaven doing his will, fighting his battles.

These dramatic images of God as the Lord of heavenly powers are descriptions of God in conflict. In the Bible that is most of the time. God doesn't sit in heaven manipulating events on earth like a puppetmaster. He is at war. His enemies are human corruption and injustice, falsity and pride. His allies are not those who hold great power on earth but the poor and the weak and the exploited. God may be almighty but he certainly isn't completely in control. On the contrary, God seeks, and needs, the active co-operation of his people. Time and again God challenges his people. He calls men and women to fight for him, reluctant and unwilling as they often are. He storms against those who worship him, threatening and assaulting them with various disasters. Worship is not enough. They must act. Even when they fail to respond God does not give up on them. He does not sweep them away in a fit of destructive fury but tries again and again to communicate his will and his hope. Nothing but action and commitment will do. God's will for the earth is not simply established by divine commandment. It requires a human response to come to its fulfilment.

The only place in the Bible where God is described as being almighty in the sense of being omnipotent is in the book of Revelation. At the end of the world 'the Lord God reigns omnipotent'. But that is after the judgement, when the conflicts of human history have been resolved. The resolution comes, not by divine overruling, but by the slow and painful growing together of God and man. The co-operation between God and man is a risky and difficult business for both sides. It leaves many tragic ambiguities in history and personal experience. But the end result is assured. God will be all in all, and this triumph will include the full flowering and coming to maturity of men and women. This weaving together of the divine and the human has already begun. The perfect balance of divine initiative and human response has already been achieved in human life, in the life of Jesus. This life has left its indelible mark and challenge on the human race. By his life of obedience to God's will, even in the face of unbearable pain and sorrow, Jesus has become the standard of human possibility, the interpreter of human destiny.

So, just as the creeds' description of God as 'Father' pointed us towards the 'Son', so do the creeds' description of God as 'almighty' point us to the one whose life was marked by obedience, who ended his life totally powerless, pinned to a cross of barren wood.

Creator

Lastly the creeds describe God as creator. He is the creator of heaven and earth, and of all that is, seen and unseen. God is the original from whom all draw being. Behind the existence of this universe, and of any other universes that there have been or might be is the initiative of the divine will.

For many people belief in God starts and ends here. It is natural to assume that if God is the creator of all that is, there should be some evidence of his creative work. Some feel that the sheer fact that there is anything at all requires God as an explanation. But most modern philosophers reject that argument. There is no reason why the fact of existence should require an ultimate explanation. The universe might simply *be*. Some feel that there is evidence for God in the order of nature and in the emergence of life and the evolution of consciousness out of lifeless matter. But science has shown us that the natural order does not need a divine designer and that the origin of life and the evolution of consciousness can be understood without reference to God. Naturalistic explanations are neater and more economical than those involving God.

There are religious people who find this rather shocking because they are moved to awe by the intricacy and splendour of the universe and find themselves overwhelmed by the certainty that there must be a God behind it all. But that is because we inherit a tradition which interprets nature as God's handiwork. The Christian may well turn this sense of awe into worship and praise of God as creator. But awe is not evidence. Nature itself is ambiguous. The universe exhibits beauty and terror, symmetry and randomness. It certainly isn't a chaos, but there aren't many clear-cut signs of purpose either. There is too much that is random, arbitrary, waste and subject to chance.

The religious puzzle about nature is not just a modern problem. It was felt centuries before the rise of modern science and philosophy and was expressed most clearly in the teachings attributed to the Indian teacher, Gautama, who lived in the sixth century before Christ. Gautama grew up in a society which acknowledged a creator god as the maker of heaven and earth. Gautama was a religious rebel – he was not impressed with the creator. He did not see much sign of purposeful design in the universe. What was more obvious to him was universal frustration. Everything was in process of endless and repeated change. This process was fuelled by a desperate craving for existence. The craving acted like a destructive fire, an unassuageable longing for permanence and stability which could never be satisfied. Everywhere there was evidence of this frustration; in the relentless facts of birth, change, ageing and death. If there were divine beings, Gautama reckoned, they were as much part of this process as everything else. All beings, gods included, needed a way out. Gautama became known as the 'Buddha', which means the 'enlightened one'. Buddhism is the way out which he taught – a religious practice aimed at stopping the frustration at its root of craving, and passing beyond the taints of existence into the peace of extinction. Buddhism is a kind of atheism which arose as a protest against too facile a concept of God as creator.

So how do the creeds stand up in their claim that God is the creator against the stern religious protest of Buddhism and the dismissive criticisms of science and philosophy where God is no longer found to be necessary?

I believe that we must begin by acknowledging the force of these arguments. If God is the creator then he has hidden himself within the processes of creation. We come to understand him as creator, not directly through nature, not even *directly* through the fact of human existence, but by another route altogether.

This other route is indicated in the Bible. The Bible begins with a solemn account of the creation of heaven and earth: 'In the beginning God created the heavens and the earth . . .' But, though this comes at the beginning of the Bible, it is by no means the oldest or earliest part of the Old Testament. What it reflects may go back very early into the most primitive of myths but, in the form we have it here, it is a sophisticated repetitive account composed by religious experts. It is not an explanation, but an affirmation and a response to the reality of God.

The Hebrews didn't get to the idea of God as creator by looking at the stars and sunset and wondering what lay behind it all. They started somewhere quite different. The reality of God broke in on them in their own history and experience. A band of Hebrew slave labourers in Egypt experienced what they understood as divine rescue. The God who set them free was a mystery. He helped them to escape and bound them to himself at the holy mountain of Sinai, promising them a prosperous future in return for their loyalty. It took the Hebrews years to develop a full 'theology'. Gradually they came to associate their God Yahweh with the religious myths and sagas of their past. When they achieved the conquest of Canaan and settled there, adopting such institutions as the monarchy, their faith developed again in broader directions. But it was the memory of the desert that lay at the root of their faith – to which they were recalled by the great books of the law and by the prophets. The god of the desert was a mystery; an angry, passionate and frightening god. At first the Hebrews probably believed in a number of divine beings. Yahweh was their special god and he demanded of them an absolute allegiance. His name was too dreadful to be spoken, he could not be represented in images. Nothing was to be worshipped as a symbol for him. Yahweh forbade even mild expressions of piety to the agricultural deities, to wind or rain or sun. The Israelites were to depend on him and him alone. Out of this austere and sometimes violent faith came the mature Jewish belief in 'One God'. The Jews believed that the lord Yahweh was not just 'their' God, not even that he was the most powerful of gods, but that he was the only God. Everyone's God. The Creator of all that is.

So, in the Bible, belief in God as creator stands at the end of a long process of discovery and not, as we might think, at the beginning. The God declared as creator by the creeds is not an abstract God who fits a gap left in our understanding, or fills in the bits that science can't yet explain. He is not a necessity of human thought or a deduction from detached observation. He is recognized as creator after, and not before, he is experienced as saviour. Only after he reveals himself in the depths of our experience can we begin to reflect on his activity in creation. On its own the universe remains an ambiguity, full of death, chance and beginning; disorder, delight, waste and abundance.

This way of thinking about God as the one revealed in our experience is not confined to the Bible and the creeds. It is found in many religions and among those who are suffocated by conventional religion – and seek God outside it. At this point we need to underline a distinction which we have already begun to notice. There is a distinction between belief in God which is superstitious and belief in God which is religious.

Superstition and religion[2]

Superstitious beliefs are those that are based on 'evidence' and look for 'results'. The superstitious believer looks to God for explanations, for authority. The God of superstition sanctions human morality and social codes. This God lies behind all religions of convention. He supports the *status quo*. In English churches he is worshipped at Christmas and Mothering Sunday because he supports the nuclear family and endorses the sentimentalizing of childhood. He is worshipped at Harvest because he is found in nature and on Remembrance Sunday because he is 'on our side' against our national foes.

This God is an idol. He is a safe God, a creation of our imagination, a confection of our desires and speculations. He is a God who can be manipulated by prayer. Many superstitious believers bargain with God in times of stress or sickness, as if the promises they make can somehow influence God to take away the pain of life. It is natural, it may be a way to faith, but it is not yet faith in the God of the creeds and the Bible. Just as believers try to manipulate this God, so do politicians and moralists, claiming that belief in God is good and expedient because it provides divine backing for desirable moral absolutes. But this God, this idol, does not stand up to the dark realities of human experience.

Seeing through the idols

It is not surprising that people see through this idol and reject God. They know that the pain of life is not taken away and that there are ambiguities of loving and living beyond cut and dried morality. These people feel the absence of God as a painful negative at the root of their lives. They *want* to believe, but nothing that is on offer seems able to satisfy their want. 'I wish I *could* believe', they say. But when they look at the cosiness and self-righteousness that often goes with conventional belief they know it's not for them. Better the darkness of the absence of God than a false security. It is often assumed that religion originated in superstition and has only become relatively refined and sophisticated in modern times. Anthropologists of the last century thought that man invented religion to explain things he couldn't understand, or to help control his fears of the dark and of death. Modern anthropologists find this view simplistic. Though there are superstitious elements in all religion, modern and ancient religion have a great deal in common. Religious belief, as opposed to superstition, is a response to something deep. It is something so deep that it cannot be expressed in any other way than by religion. It resists and evades all attempts to define it or categorize it or explain it away. This is the kind of religion that is formed in the desert where no images or names are allowed. It arises for Christians today precisely at the point where they realize that superstitious religion has died for them leaving a vast emptiness. It is to this emptiness that the creeds speak. This is because their God is the God of the Bible and the desert who proclaims himself over, against and in opposition to all human attempts to manipulate and control him.

And here we come up against another reason why the religion of the creeds is so unpopular. The God of the creeds cannot be understood or contained by the human mind. The God of the creeds will not fit neatly into the spaces made for him. He will not speak to our agenda. If he comforts us, and satisfies us in our search for faith he also opens us to the vastness of his reality; discomforts and unsatisfies us so that we are forced to give up or go on seeking.

The God of the creeds is neither safe nor tidy. He is a big God, without face or name or shape. He is a difficult God to live with as all religions of revelation have found.

Judaism, Christianity and Islam all worship the same God. And for all of them he is a God who rejects idols. In Judaism the ban on idolatry is expressed in the first two of the ten commandments. Idolatry is also forbidden in the Koran. When Abraham the patriarch responds to the call of God and sets out from the pagan city of Ur, the Koran describes him smashing all the idols in his father's house. The New Testament stresses again and again that the barriers of the old religion have been taken down and that there is no restriction to the activity of God, or his passionate purpose for human beings.

Yet all the religions, in their different ways, have failed to live with this big, strange God. It has proved impossible for religion to free itself entirely from superstition. Indeed, superstition may be a necessary stage on the way to faith. At the same time it is recognized again and again that superstition is an obstacle to mature faith which obscures the true nature of God. And it isn't only superstition that can get in the way of the experience of God. Religion needs to codify experience in order to hand it on while keeping in touch with its historic roots. The creeds are part of this code, as are all sorts of religious laws, institutions and practices. There is always a danger that the code becomes a substitute for God – the map, as it were, is mistaken for the territory.

Those who believe in the God revealed in the Bible have to live with this tension. It is the tension of the desert faith and it can never be wholly relieved or assuaged. Believers in God are pilgrims and they must be prepared to ditch religious baggage when it gets in the way. Once this tension is accepted it becomes a springboard of energy. Belief in God as the one beyond all imagined and imaginable horizons becomes a source of human healing. It gives a depth and perspective to the things that happen to us. It is a cool reminder to us of our mortality, and also a strength in which we can face the fact that we will die. A sense of the hugeness of God, contrasted with our brevity and weakness saves us from self-importance and self-dramatization.

But there is also in the tension of belief a great deal which baffles and bewilders us. There is cruelty, as well as glory, in the huge God of the Bible. His reality looms over human kind with pity for our weakness. But he is so far from us that we are forbidden to think him or name him or identify him. We are utterly vulnerable to him but his face is hidden from us. What does he want from us, why does he hide himself when we need him most? Why do we experience him as Absence as well as – or even more often than – Presence? It is not surprising that religious people become fatalistic, accepting everything that happens as part of the Almighty's inscrutable will. We need some way of asking God our deep questions and some way of comprehending what it is that he wishes to communicate to us. Suffering under the tension of belief in God, all religions seek for a focus which makes faith more bearable. The focus acts like a two-way mirror, reflecting earth to heaven and heaven to earth. The focus does not come after the revelation of the desert as an afterthought. It springs from the desert itself, from the very harshness and abruptness of God's manifestation of him-self in history. The focus is in each religion the protection against the evasions of superstition and idol making. The focus differs in Christianity, Judaism and Islam. But its essential character is that of WORD.

The Word of God – Islam

In Islam, the faith which retains most consciousness of its desert roots, the Word of God is identified with the Koran. The Koran is much more than an inspired scripture. The words themselves are eternal. They are the speech of God, the final utterance of his will. The speech of God was revealed to Muhammad, God's prophet, by the angel Gabriel on a holy mountain. Muhammad, in receiving God's words, did not edit or interpret or question them. His role was to receive and transmit. Today when Muslims use the Koran they do not read it, as religious people might read an instructive text, they read it ritually so that the actual Arabic words and their sounds penetrate the personality. The Word of God, as the Koran in Islam, is one-way speech from God to man. The response from man to God is one of obedience, gratitude and discipline. Men and women are to submit themselves to the will of God, recalling it constantly in ritual prayers and observance. It is true, of course, that not every detail of human behaviour is dealt with in the Koran, and there is room for human interpretation. Islam needs lawyers, and its clergy are lawyers, for areas of dispute need to be settled according to traditional principles. However, the point of all interpretation is to keep Muslims faithful to the revealed will of God. The word Islam means 'submission'.

The Word of God – Judaism

In Judaism the emphasis is different. In the Hebrew scriptures there are stories about men and women and God communicating with each other as *friends*, in spite of the weakness of man and the overwhelming hugeness of God. Old Testament heroes are visited by angels who are interpreted as manifestations of God himself. Jacob the patriarch dreams of a ladder linking heaven and earth and wrestles all night with a divine stranger who leaves him wounded and blessed. Men and women are allowed to question God even though this questioning sparks off the divine anger. Moses, after the overwhelming revelation of God at the burning bush rejects God's call to him: 'Oh my Lord, send I pray, some other person.' Through these stories and legends a rather different picture of God emerges. It is of one who desires man, and can be rejected by man. The word of God comes to men and women in the form of law, and the law is a great gift to be celebrated and enjoyed.

50

This law, 'Torah' as it is in Hebrew, has a wide range of meaning. It applies to God's special people, the Jews, and regulates their religious and social life. It also includes the broader principles which affect all human action. Even more widely, Torah is seen as the regulating principle running through the whole of creation. Human and animal life, stars, seasons and tides, all follow Torah. But Torah is not just something laid down at the creation. It is continually being made, adapted and interpreted afresh. Torah is made in the dialogue, debate and argument between God and man. Jews are not afraid to argue with God. Part of this argument comes out of the historic experience of the Jews. As a people they have been through appalling periods of exile and suffering. And it is right in Judaism to question God about his will and his work. In their tradition Jews sometimes win.

The Word of God – as person

Christianity inherits the Hebrew scriptures. It also inherits Jesus, a Jew of his own time. Christianity is closer to Judaism than Islam. But in identifying the focus which links heaven and earth, in finding forms for the Word of God, it goes much further than either Judaism or Islam. It goes so far and is so extreme that it changes and expands the whole idea of God. Jews and Muslims have always recognized this, and see in Christianity a deep threat to the fundamental belief in one God which all three faiths claim to share.

The focus in Christianity is still called Word, but it is word, not in the form of a book, or law or dialogue, but word as 'flesh', as person. This person is a divine person, embodying the divine presence towards men and women, both the bigness, the strangeness and the friendliness of God. He also expresses the response to God and the searching and striving of men and women who seek God. Human beings cannot live with the true God, nor can they live without him. They cannot endure the God who cannot be known by reason or held by emotion. They become distracted and diverted into superstition and idolatry. Those who protest and become atheists are equally vulnerable to self deception. But belief in God's Word made Flesh triggers a whole new vision of God and life which is at the core of Christian experience.

It is to this core, encapsulated in the creeds that we now turn. We might reflect as we do so that it is not the big and important

51

words of the creeds that are necessarily the most interesting, but the little words which make the links. We come to the end of the first set of things the creeds want to say about God. Then we start again. We declare our faith in God

And in one Lord Jesus Christ . . .

There comes a point in the Christian recitation of faith where we abandon our incomplete statements about God and start again:

I believe . . .
We believe . . .

NOTES

1 Paul Davies, *God and the New Physics*, (Dent 1983).
2 This section owes a good deal to the writings of D. Z. Phillips, particularly *Religion Without Explanation*, (Blackwell 1976).

4

MY DANCING DAY

We believe in one Lord, Jesus
    Christ, the only Son of God,
eternally begotten of the Father,
God from God, Light from Light,
true God from true God,
begotten, not made,
of one Being with the Father.
Through him all things were made.
For us men and for our salvation
he came down from heaven;
by the power of the Holy Spirit
he became incarnate of the Virgin
    Mary, and was made man.
For our sake he was crucified
    under Pontius Pilate;
he suffered death and was buried.

On the third day he rose again
in accordance with the Scriptures;
he ascended into heaven
and is seated at the right hand of
    the Father.
He will come again in glory
to judge the living and the dead,
and his kingdom will have no end.

I believe in Jesus Christ, his
    only Son, our Lord.

He was conceived by the power of
    the Holy Spirit
and born of the Virgin Mary.

He suffered under Pontius Pilate,
was crucified, died, and was
    buried.
He descended to the dead.
On the third day he rose again.
He ascended into heaven,
and is seated at the right hand
    of the Father.
He will come again to judge the
    living and the dead.

❧❧❧

Tomorrow shall be my dancing day
I would my true love did so chance
To see the legend of my play
To call my true love to my dance
Sing O my love, O my love, my love, my love
This have I done for my true love.[1]

I
A Definition, a Story and a Diagram

The second section of the creed is the longest. It is an unwinding of the central theme of Christian faith, the person and the work of Jesus Christ.

Definition

At the beginning, the subject, Jesus Christ, is identified. In the Apostles' creed the definition is relatively simple. Jesus Christ is defined as 'his [God's] only Son, our Lord'. In the Nicene creed the definition is much longer, more elaborate and repetitive. This is because it reflects an acute controversy over the identity of Jesus Christ which split the church in the fourth century. The Nicene description is close to poetry or worship; Jesus Christ is 'God from God, Light from Light, true God from true God'.

In both creeds the definition of Jesus Christ is in uncompromisingly divine terms. Jesus Christ is presented as a divine person, who comes from God the Father. The Nicene creed goes as far as to say that Jesus is most intimately connected to the Father – he is not 'made' by the Father, as part of creation, but 'begotten', fathered by him and 'of one Being' with him. In astonishingly simple but utterly mysterious and baffling words the Nicene creed goes on to assert that all the Father's creative acts have taken place through the divine Son: 'Through him all things were made.'

A story

The creeds go on to tell a story. The divine person, Jesus Christ, has a history. Just as we might record the highpoints of a person's life noting such things as birth, education, marital status, work, interests, descendants and death; so the creeds plot the high points of the divine history, stating that he 'came down from heaven', 'became incarnate of the Virgin Mary', 'was made man', 'was crucified', 'suffered death and was buried', 'rose ...', 'is seated ...', 'will come again ...' Much of this is baffling to us. We have no way of verifying whether or not the divine son of God 'came down from heaven'. But part of his history is squarely inside our recorded human history. The creeds assert that Jesus Christ 'suffered under Pontius Pilate'.

Pontius Pilate was a real Roman governor who held authority over the province of Judaea from AD 26 to AD 36. The history of

54

the divine person, identified in the creeds as Jesus Christ, here coincides with human history and human geography. In the detail of his death the divine history touched firm, recordable human ground. The life and career of Pontius Pilate, his successes and failures, are open to our scrutiny. During his governorship, the creeds assert, Jesus Christ 'was crucified, died and was buried'.

A diagram

In the Nicene creed the history of the divine person is presented almost in pictorial terms. It is in the shape of a parabola. The history of Jesus Christ is like a line that comes from the top of the page, swings in a curve when it hits what represents 'earth', and reaches its lowest point beneath the earth. Then the line curves upwards again and ends up back where it started. Everything that happens to Jesus Christ, and everything that he does between the two 'heavenly' ends of the parabola is 'for us men and for our salvation'. The divine history unfolds in response to human need.

What are we to make of this? What are the human needs to which Jesus Christ speaks? What is it that the writers and compilers of the creeds believed we needed to be saved from?

II
'For Us Men and for Our Salvation'

The Apostles' creed says nothing directly about 'salvation'. The Nicene creed mentions it in passing, as it were, as the reason for the unfolding of the divine history.

'Salvation' is a word with many meanings. It embarrasses some people who think it is a word only used by those with a rather emotional approach to religion who have a taste for brass bands or massed gospel choirs. Salvation in the Bible has to do with God's purpose. It is what he wills for his creation. It is the defeat of all that endangers and threatens what God has made. It is the vindication and completion of his work. If you don't like the word try 'fulfilment', 'final security', 'peace' or 'wholeness'. None of them are as rich or subtle as salvation, but all contain aspects of what is meant by it.

Salvation can be applied broadly or narrowly. It can refer to one person making their peace with God or to the whole universe as it rolls into glory. The pressure of God and his intention for the works of his hands are the same. But what about 'us men'?

Salvation and us

We have already seen how the bigness and strangeness of God force us to seek a third term, a 'Word' that will speak of him to us and of us to him. We also have problems with each other, which cause us to seek for help. We are frequently forced to be aware of the hostility which separates members of the human species from one another. We speak of the 'barriers' which divide people, which prevent them from 'getting through' to each other. We speak of relationships 'breaking down', suggesting that what holds people or groups together is easily capable of collapse under pressure.

What causes these barriers and pressures is inequality of power. In any human relationship one side is going to be stronger in some aspect than the other. There is always a threat of exploitation or oppression. Men, women, parents, children, races, classes, states, powers and superpowers are all engaged in a constantly shifting and changing play of power. The play is not always conducted with threats and missiles. It can be conducted with charm, diplomacy, tact, common sense, compassion and wisdom. But power play it is all the same. It originates in our deepest and earliest struggle. The struggle for survival.

Survival – 'selfish genes'

We start with biology. Other members of our species, and other whole species, are in competition with us for the means of life. Life is driven by the urge to replicate. Life feeds off life, and the race goes to those individuals and their descendants who are best able to adapt to their environment.

Human beings, like other life forms, are driven by their 'selfish genes'. Even though, in order to survive, we sometimes need to co-operate with others, at the root of this apparent altruism is the self-interest of biology. We seek power over others, or live under the protection of others, in order to further our genetic interests. This is not, of course, the whole story. But it is enough of it to place us in considerable doubt about each other's intentions.

The balance of human power is never stable. And hence we are doomed to live in a state of tension and insecurity with each other. This tension keeps us alert and watchful for threats. Our trust in each other is nearly always provisional. Anxiety triggers our most strenuous efforts to dominate others or to find safety for ourselves and those who share our genes from others' violence.

We have, as a race of intelligent beings, proved notoriously successful at defending and protecting ourselves. So successful in fact that we have created ultimate weapons. Ultimate weapons require us to label those we do not trust as ultimate enemies. So our success has brought us to a point of great danger. If God wants the human race to come to salvation something has to happen to redeem the problems which arise from our biology.

Survival – blood relations

We can also look at the problem of power from an emotional standpoint. Just as we seem unable to live with God and unable to live without him; so our human relationships are character-ized by dependency and revolt.

We are born into dependency. Each individual is a fruit of the mystery of human sex. The act of sex in which we were con-ceived may have been impelled by love or loneliness, violence or forgetfulness. Our existence may have been passionately desired by our parents, or it may have been deeply regretted. It may have been the result of chance, whim, accident or cruelty. Before we are born we are not our own. We are part of a struggle for power and survival.

The human family marks us for life. We are formed, emotion-ally, by the horrors and delights of family life. Families are where we learn love and hate, affection and jealousy, shame and self-respect. Family bonds are the most powerful of bonds, and their distortion is lethal poison.

The ambiguity of the family has always been recognized. The myth of Cain and Abel in the book of Genesis portrays the first murder as a fratricide, the result of uncontrollable jealousy be-tween brothers. The myths and tragedies of the ancient Greeks explore the potential violence under the surface of our closest relationships. Oedipus murders his father and marries his mother. Agave tears her son, Pentheus, to shreds in a Bacchic orgy. Neither know what they are doing, they are both ignorant of their victim's identity. Knowledge, to Oedipus, is the darkest revelation, he blinds himself, unable to bear the world of light.

Our own experience confirms the fact that the family which nurtures us can also set the pattern of our ruin. The human family is a world of distorted perceptions and failed love. The mistakes that we have been born into we seem condemned to repeat, one generation after another. Yet the family still contains a promise. Most of us, however awful our own experience has been, opt to repeat it. We marry and have children, hoping to play a part in the making of a truly 'happy' family. We go on believing that human love can be a true and lasting gift. We renew our instinctive faith in the possibility of fulfilment through love.

So the family draws us, with its curse and promise. We cannot live without it and we cannot live with it. Even if we turn our backs on family life and opt for solitude, promiscuity or some alternative structure of living, the imprinting of our earliest years continues to govern our emotional reactions. We seem doomed to work out our inheritance, for good or ill.

If our families have deprived us of love we may find that our other relationships reflect a desperate search for the security and acceptance of which we have been robbed. If we have been smothered by possessive or over-protective love we may spend our lives running away from the emotional demands that others make of us.

Chase and flight, losing and finding, estrangement and homecoming are the ingredients of romantic love. They carry, as we know, a promise and a curse, and for those who are able to stick it out, a promise beyond the curse. Sexual love is a game and a chase, a search for likeness within unlikeness, for recognition in a strange and forbidden country. Sexual love holds out the promise of transformation. Yet it also betrays, turns out to be a cheat and a disappointment. We are cast up on the seashore of our own aloneness, alone with unassuageable pain.

The longing, the promise, the disappointment and subsequent grief or anger, the resources for endurance, the capacity or incapacity for forgiveness and the recovery of hope are transmitted from parents to children in the coded messages of the emotions.

Emotional messages come through as strong and clear as the messages carried by the genes; and, like genes, the basic emotional patterns are selfish, they have to do with survival. Emotions are the inherited weapons of response to a world that is both entrancing and dangerous. Through the control or un-control of emotion we consciously or unconsciously seek power over others, to keep them in their place, either as our protectors or, as enemies, at a safe distance.

Unlike genes, though, the emotional patterns we inherit as individuals are capable of transformation through our personal attention to them. To that transformation, love is the key. Human love and divine love, divine love *in* human love, human love transfigured by the love of God.

The need to survive, biologically and emotionally, has turned us out as delightful, perverse, mysterious beings, who desire, and are frustrated, and go on hoping. Hopelessly selfish, we yet remain unsatisfied with all the satisfactions of the self.

Survival – codes of law

Human beings, in common with other species, have evolved social codes which help them to live with one another. Law, whether it takes the form of custom, taboo or sophisticated codification helps to compensate for some of the dangerous inequalities in our relationships. It helps to make the unbearable more bearable.

The universal taboo against incest is a good example. It is recognized that for a parent to have sex with its own offspring is an abuse of power with potentially dangerous consequences. Law gives us a means, in a rough and violent world, to regulate some aspects of our behaviour. It helps us to decide the point at which violence becomes unacceptable and what needs to be done to restore equilibrium.

Law is so important that it is often vested with deep religious significance. It is seen as part of God's speech to us, as we have seen. But law doesn't drop from heaven as a finished product. Human beings are creative law-makers, and law-breakers! The moral person believes in the goodness of law and tries to live from principle. But there is no guarantee, of course, that this will succeed. Good people are frequently betrayed by the unscrupulous. Goodness does not always equal happiness. Worse, good people are sometimes betrayed by their own goodness. Their own compassion, or care, or wisdom lead them into impossible dilemmas. Virtue can be its own downfall as well as its own reward.

The unscrupulous person may be caught out and punished for his crimes. But his demise is not tragic, it is appropriate. Those who are betrayed by their own strengths *are* tragic, however. They reveal a flaw in the pattern of our being for which there seems to be no healing.

Law, then helps us to live. We cannot live without it. It is a mercy and a blessing, which is why the Jews celebrate Torah as God's greatest gift. But law cannot of itself unlock the doors of our perceptions. It cannot create compassion for the weak, or transform hatred and jealousy into understanding. It cannot of itself untie the knots of our dilemmas, probe our psychological wounds, change the patterns of genetic selection or vindicate the victims of moral tragedy.

Still, law reminds us that things are not as they should be, and that they could be other. Law is a protest against human violence and lust for power. It is a place of dialogue between God and man. In the creation of law God and man became vulnerable to each other, to argument, pity and persuasion.

Within the Jewish understanding of Torah there is a protest at the limitations of law itself. It is recognized that law must go beyond itself. It cannot just be imposed externally, it must spring from the human heart. From the Christian point of view, law is the anticipation of the gospel. It prepares for the outbreak of love.

Helplessness

Christianity assumes that what is wrong with us is serious. The pressures on our nature have bound us to a condition of inherited helplessness and danger. Law, as codes or conventions, has acted down the centuries as a breakwater, saving us from being swamped by our own violence. But today, in the age of nuclear terror, law and convention are in danger of being overridden. An accident, a misunderstanding, could trigger a nuclear exchange which could annihilate life on this planet. We need to remember again and again that we are not wholly rational beings, and that, by denying the irrational part of ourselves we are more likely to be possessed by it.

I have stressed the more depressing aspects of our helplessness for a reason. It has become commonplace in recent years for Christians to underplay the dark side of human experience. Guilt and sin are problems. They cause, in Christian circles, a certain amount of embarrassment. Hearty denials of sin are coupled with a stress on the positive. The Victorians, convent schools, the Tridentine Mass and the Book of Common Prayer are all frequently blamed, rightly or wrongly, for perpetuating a rather morbid and damaging version of Christianity.

Horror stories abound from gloomy vicarages, dim confessionals and dark Calvinist chapels. That there have been distortions cannot be doubted. But something else has been going on as well.

A recipe for happiness?

In recent years Christians have tended to present their faith as a recipe, if not for success, at least for human happiness and fulfilment. The positive and optimistic side of experience has been well to the fore. There has been a tendency to leave the more negative side, which manifests as guilt, pride and depression to the 'secular' healers: to doctors, counsellors, psychotherapists, and, if all else fails, to the Samaritans.

In presenting the gospel as a recipe for happiness, and sloughing off the dark side to 'the professionals', Christians have not, I believe, been offering a critique of inadequate theologies so much as colluding with the assumptions and expectations of our success-based society. In such a climate Christians are vulnerable to the pressure to have to have something to offer. That 'something' must be positive – so, the 'selling' of the gospel as 'inner peace', 'wholeness', or 'purpose'. All these are clearly desirable, like enough money, good health, and interesting work.

But the gospel, sold in terms of emotional and social benefits, doesn't always deliver. The impact of the Christian message on an individual or a community may be to stir up a lot of fear, darkness, guilt and dread. There may be years of wounding and damage to be recognized and owned. Not for nothing is the intrusion of God into the lives of individuals in the Bible often preceded by the comforting words, 'Fear not'. There is plenty to be afraid of from the big, strange God of biblical faith, and it is a characteristic human response to flee or hide. Other ploys are to remind the divine visitor of one's youth (Jeremiah), handicap (Moses), sinfulness (Isaiah), sexual inexperience (Mary), or anything else which makes one in one's own eyes an unsuitable candidate for the divine involvement.

Inner peace, purpose and wholeness may be desirable, but in Christian faith the primary encounter is with the mystery of God. This is ultimately healing and hopeful for us – hence the 'fear not'. But the gospel is not a tranquillizer. It is surgery, radical and devastating. The whole stress of the Christian diagnosis is that we are in a condition where we *cannot* help ourselves. What is wrong with us is *us*. The problem is not in our circumstances, or even in our perceptions, but in the deep structures of our being.

This may seem pessimistic. But it also contains deep hope. The hope is that change is possible for us. And not only possible, but willed and intended by the one who originally willed us into existence.

'For our salvation' – the different religions

All religions recognize that our problem is with ourselves, with what we inherit and what we transmit. All speak of salvation and offer paths of transformation. Some religions work the transformation from the outside inwards, others from the inside outwards.

Religions which place great stress on law are working from the outside inwards. Men and women are seen as free, if sometimes rather unruly, agents of divine purpose. Salvation is for them to find themselves within the will of God. The wayward part of human nature is to be brought, consciously and diligently, under the control of law. The stress is on obedience. The passions and instincts are to be brought to submission. Law is not only instruction. It is also consolation. It affirms that God really is in control, in spite of appearances of the contrary. Islam, Judaism, Sikhism and some forms of Hinduism are strong in these elements.

Christianity also recognizes the role of law, as we have seen. But it asserts that what is most wrong with us is what we can't help. This is 'original' sin, the wrongdoing that we are unable to recognize because it springs from wounds we have received in our making. It is bias, distortion, that we cannot see in ourselves. But we can, and do, see it in others, as they see it in us. So we punish and deprive each other, not realizing that we, too, are imprisoned by false perspectives.

Law, in Christian understanding, helps to control the effects of original sin. But control is not the same as healing.

Other religious traditions recognize this. They seek salvation from the inside outwards. The path of transformation is through introspection. By observing the inner processes of the mind and heart the seeker acquires a measure of detachment from his unruly nature. He comes to appreciate some of the causes of distorted thinking. There may be moments of sudden, devastating illumination. There may be years of slow, patient discovery.

Either way the individual self is slowly unravelled, rather as an onion is peeled away. The unravelling is an unmasking of illusions and self-deceptions. Eventually the seeker reaches a point where the consciousness of being a separate self vanishes. At this point he has reached salvation. He is free. Some schools of Hinduism, most forms of Buddhism, classical Taoism and a number of spiritual disciplines based on a combination of Eastern teachings and psychotherapy stress the inner way.

Christianity, too, has its traditions of meditation. It recognizes the need to go inward. Illusions must be stripped away with patient truthfulness. But the purpose, in Christianity, is not to annihilate the self, but to open it, layer and layer, to the source of its being, God. At the end of the search is not a nothing but a presence. This discovery drives the Christian disciple back again and again into the external world. What is discovered at the core of the self as the love and compassion of the Creator must be affirmed in the world of the neighbour and the enemy.

Christian salvation is a process and a movement. We go deeper and deeper within, guided by the Scriptures, to find the source of our being. We return again and again to retell the good news in whatever tongues we are given.

The remaking of persons

Christian salvation is about the remaking of persons at all levels; biological, emotional and moral. We can unlock the content of salvation in each of these directions.

We can see salvation as a massive source of energy and hope at a point of crisis in our evolutionary development. We can see it as a source of healing for our personal wounds and a means of transforming our injuries into compassion for others. We can see it as the undisclosed answer to our experience of tragedy. It is directed not only to life in this world, but to those whose griefs are inconsolable in this life.

Our part in salvation is to recognize our need for it and be open to what is given. This sounds unbelievably simple. It may offend us because it puts us in the position of being passive recipients rather than being active achievers. But, as we know, there is an art in receiving, which is very far from being merely passive, that requires our deepest attention and concern. The need to receive is obvious in the cases of 'biological' and 'moral' salvation. Either God can do something about our selfish genes or he can't.[2] Either God can vindicate the victims of tragedy beyond this life or he can't.

But the issue is more complex when we look at our personal wounds and sins.

Salvation and the art of archery

The word 'sin' in Christian teaching comes from a Greek word which means 'missing the mark'. It's a word that reminds us of the art of archery. Archery is a graceful sport. It depends on natural co-ordination and instinct. Archers can learn *technique*, but success depends in the end on innate skills.

In the Zen school of Buddhism, archery and other sports are practised almost as contemplative disciplines. The Zen archer aims to hit the mark not by conscious striving but by calling on his natural skill. He needs to bring body and mind into harmony. Raw energy and instinctive skill are to be balanced in effortless tension. From effortless tension comes the ability to draw the bow spontaneously, and hit the target.

Sin is a failure in a natural skill – the skill of being. Christian tradition has sometimes over-emphasized the moral aspects of sin. It has assumed either that human beings are innately evil (though it has done this less often, I suggest, than it is fashionable for Christians today to suppose), or that sin is a matter of conscious moral choice. Nice people *don't*.

But 'missing the mark' is something that we cannot help. We haven't developed the proper skills to hit the target spontaneously. That we do have these skills deep within our human potential is implied by the doctrine that we are made, men and women, 'in the image and after the likeness of God'. God does not lack the skill of being, the effortless balance of energies through which he performs his will.

When Christians stress the moral aspects of sin they are stressing something which feeds our pride. If sin is primarily a matter of conscious choice then choosing to avoid certain sins makes us feel superior. So, paradoxically, does the choice to commit certain sins, as long as they are interesting, intractable, or safe in the past of a mis-spent youth.

Taking the moral aspect out of sin actually makes it more serious. For then sin is a problem of being, not doing. Sin is something, not that we control, but that controls us. It is itself a sickness that we need to be healed from. The source of sin is in the wounds we have received in our making. Corporately and individually we are damaged. In the places where we are most vulnerable we have built our strongest defences. From our

64

wounds we have built weapons to clobber those who threaten us. What goes into the building of our weapons is good raw energy, the energy we need in order to survive.

Now if sin is primarily a moral problem it is manifested in what we *do*. We shall come to think that the root of it is in our energy; whether that manifests in anger, greed, lust or even in uncontrollable pleasure and delight. There is a human tendency to name the raw energy of our being as evil and to sit on it hard in the hope that it will go away. It won't. But sitting on it will mean that *we* at least won't be offended by its manifestations. Others may notice in us a certain self-righteousness, rigidity or spitefulness. But we are safe within our tower of pride.

What cracks pride is a lapse or a fall. The Garden of Eden story is the absurd tragi-comedy of the corporate 'fall' of the human race. Lapses and falls are to be welcomed, because, like Zen jokes, they shatter pride and self-reliance. They open us to the compassionate tenderness and healing love of God. There is a gentle irony in the detail of the Genesis story that God makes clothes out of animal skins for the fallen Adam and Eve.

The programme of salvation in Christianity is risky and ambitious. What is wrong with us is to be cured neither by control or excision, but by conversion. The raw energy of our being and the deep skill of being which we have lost without ever knowing it, need to be recovered and brought into harmony. Together they form the effortless tension which enables us to reach the target, the goal of our existence, the love from which and for which we were made. Or, to go back to our original metaphor, salvation is to lose ourselves and find ourselves within the dance of God. Swept into the dance it takes time to find our feet. But if we stay with the rhythm and allow ourselves to be gently guided, and sometimes roughly pushed, we shall start spontaneously to co-ordinate our movements. It takes humility though, and courage, to start. It's much easier to stay in the corner looking on – not exposing our clumsiness and ignorance.

From the prison of our pride God's love bears down on us often as threat and darkness. We fear change. We know that the power of change is not in ourselves, but in that which makes us. Yet our *consent* to change, our willed attention, is vital, since it is we who are being changed. Salvation, conversion, illumination come from outside ourselves. Yet they take effect within our nature, in the deep structures of our being. Salvation is a work of God and man. God within man.

If we are to find salvation, on all three levels; biological, emotional and moral, the whole pattern of human life, from conception to death needs to be reworked. This reworking can only come from one who not only reflects the image and likeness of God, but in some more intimate way than us, *is* the image and likeness of God. Within him the raw energy of human nature is effortlessly controlled, his skills of being have not been overridden by the need to wound others in order to survive.

Christian tradition, as summarized in the creeds, identifies the bringer of salvation as Jesus Christ, the Son of God. He is the one who comes down from heaven and reworks the whole pattern of human living and dying. He is on both sides of the great divide between man and God. He enters the blood stream of human life bringing fresh energy and hope from heaven. Unwounded in his making he is the only one in search of heaven who is able to bear and heal our wounds:

> Then was I born of a virgin pure,
> Of her I took fleshly substance.
> Then was I knit to man's nature
> To call my true love to my dance . . .

III

Jesus – Facts, Faith and Mystery

Introduction

We can see from all this that the creeds make enormous claims about Jesus Christ. They claim, that as Son of God he lived a human life and died a human death. He originates beyond our history, and yet is part of human history. This divine history touches human record 'under Pontius Pilate'. How can we believe this? None of us can stand where the first followers of Jesus stood. We have only their records to go on, and they come from faith.

The modern historian can tell us almost nothing for certain even about the human origins of Jesus. He can tell us absolutely nothing of his divine origin or destiny. Even if we scrutinize the little patch of human history which the creeds claim is a window on to the divine, we shall not find any unambiguous evidence. In the end we shall find only the reflections of our own faces, baffled, credulous or sceptical as we may be. The facts of human history do not give – either to our will to believe what the creeds say about him or to our will not to believe.

However, we should pay attention to the bare 'facts' that are available to us. They form the outline of the historian's Jesus, and they are the point of departure for most modern accounts of him. The historian's account of Jesus goes something like this:

The historian's Jesus

Jesus of Nazareth was a travelling Jewish teacher and healer. He was at first associated with a revivalist prophet, John the Baptist. Later he developed his own ministry under the pressure of a sense of divine vocation. He formed a close band of disciples. Jesus' message was like John's – a proclamation of the imminent arrival of the kingdom of God. Unlike John, whose preaching was rather sombre, Jesus stressed the joy and freedom of the kingdom.

Jesus had an intense awareness of God. He referred to God as 'Father' and used an Aramaic word which suggested that he approached God as a real son might approach a loved and trusted father. The kingdom, in the preaching of Jesus, was a new age, a party, a secret and a gift. Its coming among men and women meant a complete shake-up of the whole order of human society. The rules, values and priorities of the present age had to be reversed. Jesus used the traditional methods of Jewish teaching. He interpreted and elaborated the Jewish scriptures. He told sharp and witty and elusive stories. He denounced corruption in society and prophesied about the fate of the nation. He was also a faith healer. He interpreted his healings as a sign that the kingdom was drawing near. Even nature, and the natural processes of disease and death, rejoiced at its coming.

The Gospels show how the personality and message of Jesus divided people. Those who, for professional or social reasons, had a good deal invested in the present order of things found him intolerable. But the handicapped, the outcast, the sick, the guilty and the poor were much more receptive. They were able to see the promise of the kingdom as a gift. They heard its proclamation as good news – Gospel.

There was almost certainly a political dimension to the teaching of Jesus. He became an irritant and a threat to the religious and political hierarchy. He was regarded as a claimant to the title 'Messiah' – the chosen one of God. The showdown came in Jerusalem where Jesus seems deliberately to have provoked the opposition by staging a messianic demonstration. This was the crisis which led to his arrest, trial and death 'under Pontius Pilate'.

Hidden assumptions in the historian's account

There is nothing in the above account which is deliberately inconsistent with the creeds. But it does seem light years away from them. What has happened to the solemn language about Jesus Christ as 'God from God, Light from Light, True God from True God'?

The historian would probably reply that the creeds are about 'interpretation'. His only concern is with establishing 'the facts'. Cool and objective as such an approach seems, it contains a hidden assumption. That is, that the supernatural elements in the Gospels, the miracles, birth stories and the empty tomb are of secondary importance. If they have value, then, like the creeds, it is a secondary value. They are interesting interpretations belonging to their time. No more.

Now 'facts', as we have all been brainwashed into believing in our fact-based age, are indisputable and unproblematic. Interpretation however is secondary and arbitrary.

The theologian's Jesus

The account given above is the kind of account often presented by theologians as part of their strategy of self-explanation. It is important for them to appear to be rational and objective in their approach to 'facts'.

Most theologians, however, are also Christian believers. They read the New Testament devotionally, as well as academically, and they take part in worship, using the creeds. Though they sometimes present an unreligious view of Jesus they are still, in a sense, committed to a religious view of him in their personal lives. For many of them, though, the unreligious view dominates. This is because they believe it must be truer and more reliable because it has been arrived at by the supposedly cool, fact-finding procedures of the secular historian. The result is that they are embarrassed by the supernatural elements in the Gospels and the divine language in the creeds and feel they have to provide rational explanations for them. These explanations, plausible or not, inevitably reduce the mystery of what is claimed to what can be accommodated, without difficulty, by an intelligent unbeliever.

There are a number of ways of making the accommodation. Some claim that when the creeds describe Jesus as 'God from God' and 'Light from Light' they are using the kind of exaggerated language used of royalty or pop stars. Others claim that the supernatural stories in the Gospels are 'late', that the divine language in the creeds is a 'development' of simpler ways of believing.

Jesus really, they claim, was an inspired and great man, a man so open to the reality of God that when he spoke or acted it is, for those who follow him, *as if* God were speaking or acting. This way of coming to terms with the non-religious view of Jesus is so taken for granted by sophisticated Christians today that it is not a trivial matter to point out that it is radically at odds with the creeds, and destructive of faith.

The creeds neither deny nor contradict the purely historical account. But their assertion is that what is open to historical investigation is not all there is of Jesus, or all that can be known of him. From the unbeliever's point of view the life of Jesus can only be seen as any other life or death. What does not fit into his expectations must be ignored or explained away. Jesus was a remarkable man, but an account can be given of him which does not require a divine explanation. To the believer however it looks very different.

Faith and the mystery of Jesus

Faith finds that there is that about Jesus which *cannot* be rationally explained. Whether it is the majesty of his death, or the conviction of his aliveness after his death, whether it is his healings or teachings, his promises or contradictions, or even the magical stories of his origins, we are not dealing with something that history alone can handle. Take away the mystery, the inexplicable elements in the Gospels and you end up with a confection of our twentieth-century imagination. The core is lost.

The creeds do not *explain* the core that is missing from the historian's account. They simply state that Jesus Christ shares God's mysterious nature, his bigness, his strangeness and his friendliness. In the parabola of divine history he has descended and lived and died among us. The huge divine reality has broken itself up into the dust of the universe, forming a human person in a human womb and hiding itself in a human life and death.

God has hidden himself in Jesus Christ just as he has hidden himself in creation. Divine explanations of Jesus are not *necessary*. The 'facts' about him, the facts that a historian is interested in, do not force belief upon us. But the accounts which exclude the divine possibility somehow fail to do justice to what people find in Jesus. His ordinariness and hiddenness are important. Jesus learns to trust God within a particular tradition of teaching and faith. He has no advantages over us. The presence of God in him, his secret divine nature, is a secret even from himself. Entering the human condition in its fragmented and broken state involves God in alienation from himself. He loses himself in creation.

For Christ is God's word to us, and ours to him. God intends us to meet him in Christ on our own terms. We are to question him, to put him on trial, to tempt him, wound him and wreak on him our violence and dismay.

> Into the desert I was led
> Where I fasted without substance
> The devil bade me make stones my bread
> To have me break my true love's dance.

IV
Jesus and the Creeds

The core of the problem

The core of the problem of Jesus in the creeds has to do with his identity. How do we reconcile our limited historical knowledge of Jesus with the assertions of faith, without distorting either? How do we bring together the cautious, sober, fact-finding and rather narrow account of the historian with the enormous claims and expectations of faith?

Here we need to start looking at what the creeds say in more detail.

'One Lord – Jesus Christ'

The first creed was that 'Jesus is Lord'. 'Lord' was the name and title of Israel's God. From very early on Christian believers associated Jesus with God. St Paul, in his earliest epistles, written probably about twenty years after the death of Jesus writes of Christ as a kind of divine atmosphere. Those who believe are 'in' Christ. Just as believers in God feel surrounded by a 'presence', so the first Christians seemed to be aware of Christ surrounding and supporting them.[3]

Their awareness was quite different from that of bereaved people who 'sense' the presence of a loved one. Christ, like God, seemed to have become everywhere. He was *more* than the individual human being who some of the first disciples knew personally and intimately. The memory of the first creed, 'Jesus is Lord', is retained in our two creeds: 'I believe in Jesus Christ his only Son, *our Lord*' and 'We believe in *one Lord*, Jesus Christ . . .'

The first Christians were accused of atheism. Like the Jews they refused to acknowledge the superstitious gods of the *status quo* which were revered throughout the Roman Empire. But the taunt of atheism also stuck to them because they smashed the image most people had of God. The first Christians were aware that something deep within Judaism itself had broken down. This breakdown is associated by the New Testament writers with the death of Jesus.

'He suffered under Pontius Pilate, was crucified, died and was buried'

When Jesus was crucified, according to the account in St Mark's Gospel, darkness fell on the earth for three hours. The veil of the Jewish temple was torn in two, Mark reports, from the top to the bottom. This is powerful symbolic language. The death of Jesus plunged the earth into darkness, a darkness like the darkness before the creation of the world. Then in the darkness came an act of divine vandalism. The ritual curtain separating the holy from the profane in the holiest part of the sanctuary of the Jewish religion was torn open.

The death of Jesus as revelation

The New Testament writers seem to see the death of Jesus as a revelation. This is in itself strange. In human terms the death of Jesus was a defeat and an end. Jesus approached his death in silence. The mental anguish of his acceptance of death was seared into the memory of the disciples.

Jesus found no assurance in his death. His loving Father was not near. The big God of Judaism was not in control. Even though Jesus held on to the conviction that death was, in some way, God's will for him, it did not help him as he faced the depths of betrayal and abandonment. Jesus felt let down and tricked by God: 'My God, my God, *why* hast thou forsaken me?'

It was as though Jesus was having to endure in his own person the dislocation of all the familiar images of God. There was no longer any certainty of God's power or his love. For Jesus, it was as though there was no God. He became godless, outcast. He shared the fate of the lost, the anger of the betrayed and of all who have cried out at God, against God, at the sorrow and evil of the world.[4]

The creeds make it clear that this death was as absolute and final as any human death:

> He suffered under Pontius Pilate
> was crucified, died and was buried.
> He descended to the dead.

> He was crucified under Pontius Pilate
> He suffered death and was buried.

That is easy to grasp. The nullity of death is something we recognize even though we can't think it or imagine it for ourselves. To die is to become the past. Our present time is over. We are without a future. We are part of history.

But what happened *after* the death of Jesus is not easy to grasp. We can believe or disbelieve what the Gospels press us to believe, but we cannot *comprehend* it. Nor can we explain it without distorting its singularity:

'On the third day he rose again'

> On the third day he rose again . . .

> On the third day he rose again
> in accordance with the scriptures . . .

From the historian's point of view the only solid fact is that the disciples became convinced that Jesus was alive. They came to this conviction in a variety of different ways. The Gospel writers do little to tidy up the varying memories and stories. Between the death on the cross and the resurrection is a gap which the historian cannot handle. We are outside what can be observed and comprehended by the power of the mind. Of course, people do try to explain it rationally, as we saw in the second chapter,

72

either as a 'proof' of faith or as an 'explanation' of an unusual event.

But in the Gospels the resurrection is left untidy and unexplained. The resurrection is something unfinished, unconcluded. It brings great fear and joy, strangeness and recognition, remorse and reconciliation. The resurrection is presented as an intersecting point between earthly and heavenly reality. Jesus himself is different. He is not simply the lost one remembered and returned in the dreaming of the bereaved. He is unrecognizable. He is in an intermediate state between the Jesus they had known and the ungraspable, uncontrollable reality of God. 'Do not touch me,' he says to Mary in the garden, 'for I have not yet *ascended*.' It is in the resurrection that the disciples are forced to recognize Jesus as one whose natural environment is elsewhere. His heavenly destiny is disclosed. The risen Jesus is 'the Lord'.

Everything in the New Testament, everything in the creeds springs from this disclosure. No one had been able to romanticize the death of Jesus. He was no glorious martyr in his own cause. His agony and lostness was remembered. It was a human end. But now the disciples could see it also as a divine beginning. It was the end of one world and the beginning of another. It was a disintegration which bore fruit in new life. The new life came out of pain and blood and chaos, like any birth. Like any birth its beginning was violent and exhausting, both frail and tremendously strong. The dark revelation of the cross gave way to the bright revelation of Easter. The new life of Easter swept away the old. It inaugurated a new system of values and relationships.

The risen Jesus is the focus of the boundless love and forgiveness which flows from the heart of the Father. Through the suffering and rising of the Son of God and man issues a new world.

'He ascended into heaven and is seated at the right hand of the father'

The picture here is of Jesus as a heavenly king. He takes his seat in triumph, as a conquering hero, at the right hand of God. From there he rules the universe. His holy rule and law project out to fill all things. The picture evokes the same sort of emotions as when our local football team wins the cup final. It is carnival, it is victory, it is fun and absurd at the same time; and should not be taken entirely at face value.

At face value the ascension looks like the reinstatement of the old images of the cosmic super-king. Not now as God the Father, but as Jesus, the young prince and dragon-slayer. Ruling in splendour, dividing the complex world of human reality into goodies and baddies, answering our greedy yearning for authoritative answers. Yet the whole point of the ascension story is that it is deeply ironic. The disciples, as Luke records, have asked Jesus whether it is the time for the kingdom to be restored to Israel. If Mark were writing, the account would be phrased in such a way that we would know the disciples were being depicted as thick to the very end. But Luke is more urbane and polite and the question comes across more as pious and wistful than stupid.

However, it still reveals the continuing human fascination with the acquisition of oppressive power. Even after the death and resurrection of Jesus the disciples still look to him to give substance to their fantasies. But Jesus has no secret knowledge to give them. What they want to know, he tells them, is hidden within the mystery of the Father's will. Then, as an answer which contradicts the question, Jesus leaves them. He simply goes. The wounded, resurrected servant of God leaves those he has healed and carries his wounds into heaven.

A later generation of Christians came to think of him there in heaven, as the priest of creation, endlessly praying to the Father for those for whom he died. But the original disciples were just left to get on with it. All they could do was cheer and praise and wait. For in his parting came, not an answer to their questions, but a blessing, which was in itself a release from the compulsions of power. The disciples could no longer *see* Jesus, and they were warned against trying too hard. If they became too interested in the one who had left them behind they would miss the coming of the Spirit.

It has always been easy for Christians to become fixated on the triumphant kingly Christ. But perhaps the images and pictures of Christ in glory should be played more lightly. They are there to cheer us without making us feel superior. Jesus is not our mascot in heaven. He has entered, or rather re-entered, the orbit of his deepest being, the love of the Father from which all comes and to which all in the end returns.

What comes down from heaven now is not law or authority but Spirit. The Spirit reminds the disciples of the discoveries of Jesus as he worked through the human predicament, stage by stage. Those insights are what the disciples, then and now, have to work with.

The Spirit drove the disciples back to the Scriptures of the Old Testament to find in them the mystery of his dying and rising prefigured and foretold. The Spirit also drove them to the creation of new scriptures. It was for them to interpret the discoveries of Jesus as honestly and as faithfully as they could. It is their record which contains the mystery of his being for us, and his invitation to us in the promise of the kingdom.

'His kingdom will have no end' – law and love

What kind of a kingdom has Jesus left in the hearts of his followers? And how do its rules differ from the normal rules which govern our lives?

Law, as we have seen, is designed to protect us in our relationships with one another. Incomplete though it is, it sets limits. It requires that the limits be recognized. It marks the boundaries between the sacred and the profane, the living and the dead. It sets limits for marriage and property, for trade and commerce and government, limits for punishment and retribution. Without limits there is anarchy and moral chaos.

Jesus recognized the law in the Torah of his own tradition. But he would not be limited by it. He believed that in the new world of God's kingdom the distinctions and limits of law would no longer be necessary. That is why he welcomed the outcasts and rejects, and announced God's forgiveness to all who repented. The kingdom was the breaking in on the human race of a whole new set of possibilities. These drew their strength not from the imposition of legal boundaries but from the deeper and more dangerous energy of love.

Love is outside the law, but its strength is not anarchic. Love springs from God, as does law, but from the heart of God, his inner being. Love is about order, but it is a different sort of order from the order of law. It requires a transformation of our nature, which is part of a deeper revelation to us of the nature of God.

The implications of love and its relation to law are hinted at in the teachings of Jesus. In his teaching on marriage he acknowledges that the law allows divorce. But, says Jesus, divorce is a concession to the fact that men and women are hard-hearted. Law recognizes, rightly, that a man and a woman can come to such a degree of bitterness and death within a marriage that they need to break the relationship and start again. Law is here legislating for what is wrong with us, helping us to handle the paradoxes of our inability to live with or without each other.

Jesus, however, sees the necessity of law as a symptom of our sickness. In the kingdom of God such sickness will be cured. He saw a future for us in which law would no longer be necessary. What is wrong with us is capable of deep cure. The time will come when we will have learnt in our own nature, in the fabric of our being, how to give and receive love in ways which are not manipulative or destructive. And the time to start learning is now.

The necessity for human change is urgent in the teaching of Jesus. He called on his hearers to repent. The kingdom of God's promise could break in at any time. At any time we might find ourselves on the wrong side of the division between this age and the age to come. The values of the old age, dominated by law, are no use at all in the kingdom. All the rules have changed, and if we try to stick with the old rules we shall only stagnate or die. A crisis has come upon us. It is the crisis of God's mercy and hope.

St Paul saw this hint of crisis in the teaching of Jesus very clearly. For Paul, as for Jesus, the values of the old world were summed up in Torah. Paul does not deny the divine origin of the Torah but now, he says, it has been superseded. The law must be broken and set aside. For Paul the cross of Jesus is the breaking point. It is an act of human lawlessness in which God reveals the mercy of his own nature. To cling on to the old law in the new world makes the law an instrument of death.

This new perception of the law did not arise for Paul as a result of theological speculation. It arose for him at a point of breakdown. His conversion to Christian faith involved an emotional collapse. He came to believe that his experience was a parallel to the experiences the disciples had had of the risen Jesus. His confrontation with Jesus involved him in an experience of judgement and of healing. He was blinded and sickened by his vision. But out of it he received healing and conviction. Just as the distintegration of Jesus' life on the cross was necessary for the revelation of the resurrection, so Paul had to go through an experience of personal breakdown, a 'death' before he could respond to the gospel of grace.

'His kingdom will have no end' – the secret of relationship

The kingdom which Jesus had prophesied was opened up. His death had broken it open. And what was the secret and gift of the kingdom? It was the secret of relationship. Relationship between Jesus and the Father, relationship between Jesus and the disciples. The relationship was not based on power or contract but on love. It was based on the secret that God is not an isolated passionless God reigning in cosmic splendour. God is and always has been a relationship of love. The nameless, formless God, the one we cannot live with and cannot live without, the smasher of human images, in Jesus has a name, form, a body, a human past, speech, nationality and sexuality, hunger, laughter, grief and death. Our human sense of awe and revolt at God is changed by realizing that God is not only very big, but very small; not only vast and spiritual but earthy and natural, in the womb, embodied, and in the earth, entombed.

What finally dies on the cross is the old superstitious image of God as the cosmic overlord. The cross is death to the God who can be manipulated by man, to the God who we confect out of our fantasies, to the God whose existence can be proved and whose reality can be denied. This old God of superstition is incapable of suffering. He is too far beyond his creation to suffer in it and for it. He stands outside the world in judgement, taking his revenge on those who disobey his programme for them. This false image of God is put to death on the cross. The dying and rising of Jesus reveals a God who suffers for the world and in it to bring it to its completion. The suffering of God is an endless compassionate hurting for the world, the loving absorption of the world's darkness and dread. In Hindu religion the essential reality of God is called Brahma, which means sacrifice. We can see in the cross how God sacrifices himself for his creation. The cross is a demonstration of reality.

We can see how life feeds off life. The 'law' of our nature and of our social codes requires vengeance. The pattern written into our nature and acted out in our most fundamental relationships leads us to betrayal and murder. Yet the cross breaks the spiral and violence and counter-violence; it exhausts human fury. Only God is left at the darkness of noon on Good Friday, and God is what he always has been, inexhaustible love.

The darkness of the cross comes from the fact that it is a point of deepest conflict and creativity. Separation has entered the experience of God, it has torn God from God so that the torn fabric of the human world can be brought to healing. In the cross there is the human suffering of a human victim. There is the victim's faith in God, his unanswered prayer for deliverance, his cry of abandonment.

But that is not all. The cross is a revelation of God's nature. The one lost on the cross is the one who is to be identified as God's risen one, his son and image. The Father loses his son on the cross, he sees him die abandoned and alone. This is the cost of the Father's love for the world and his longing for it. His silence is the silence of grief and of his own commitment to see the anguish through. To respond to the son in his cry of abandonment would have been to betray the whole created universe to perdition. Like Abraham, God is prepared to sacrifice his only son for the sake of the human future. Unlike Abraham he really does it. There is no God beyond himself to appeal to, no alternative and painless sacrifice caught in a thicket.

There is a terrible contrast in the Nicene creed between the identification of Jesus and the story of his human life. The Nicene creed is the most radical and Christian statements. It declares unambiguously that Jesus Christ, the Son of God is 'of one Being with the Father'. Yet the entry of the Son of God into human life and its conclusion on the cross caused deep separation within the being of God. The body of Jesus, torn on the cross, bears this breaking within God. In the human blows and wounds, the torment of the mind and memory, the forgetfulness of all that is known and dreamed of God, God is seeking man and man is seeking God.

> Then on the cross hanged I was
> Where a spear to my heart did glance
> Then issued forth both water and blood
> To call my true love to my dance.

This is the form of God's love when it reveals itself in our fragmented and broken world. Suffering is part of what it means to be God.

'His kingdom will have no end' – suffering, love and community

Most of us have been brought up to believe that suffering is always an evil and should be avoided at all costs. But that comes partly from a failure to understand the root meaning of the word. To suffer is to be acted on by another.

Suffering becomes evil when it is imposed or inflicted on another in a way that violates love. But within love suffering is joy and fulfilment. In relationship there is always giving and receiving, action and passivity. From passivity comes 'passion'.

One is acted on by another, and 'suffers' the action of the other. Within love action and suffering are joyful and creative.

The human act of sex dimly reflects the mystery of divine love. It involves a movement and action of one upon another, a mutual giving and receiving, action and passion. In sex we imitate divine love, joyfully receiving and absorbing each other in an exchange which is fruitful.

So the cross reveals the heart of God in that it reveals the eternal relationship which is God. This revelation has immediate and practical consequences. At the foot of the cross, at least according to the Gospel of John, stand John, the disciple, and Mary, the mother of Jesus. In his dying Jesus 'gives' them to each other. They are not related, but from now on they are to live with each other and care for each other as mother and son. The cross begins a new pattern of human loving, which rises out of our release from the compulsions of power and violence.

One of the first things that happened to the disciples after the resurrection was that they became a visible community. They found in the resurrection that Jesus continued to claim them as his companions. The past and the betrayals of the past were forgiven. His heavenly identity was now manifest. But he was still their friend, more their friend because of what he had been through on their behalf. Just as he had broken bread with them 'on the night of his betrayal' when they were all about to disown and abandon him, so he broke bread with them after the resurrection. Their failures and treacheries were recognized. They were not denied but absorbed, understood and forgiven. In the breaking of bread the disciples saw again the demonstration of God's broken-ness, and of his inexhaustible love.

> Then down to hell I took my way
> For my true love's deliverance
> And rose again on the third day
> Up to my true love and the dance.

The disciples were a community. Their loyalty to each other and to their Lord was deeper and stronger than family ties or the compulsions of enmity. John, the greatest theologian of the New Testament, describes Jesus 'on the night of his betrayal' sharing his hopes for the future with his disciples. He leaves them his peace and the commandment to love. The two are connected, for peace is the fruit of love, the peace of the refusal to perpetuate our own distortions and injuries by seeking revenge on others. John describes the relationships between God and man and man and God as a cycle of love. The Son and the Father are 'in' each other. The disciples are 'in' Christ and so 'in' the Father. It is rather like a dance which originates with God the Father. It is reflected in the Son and imitated by men and women as they come gradually more and more into the orbit of God's love. The dance is a pattern of love, movement and reflection. Christ reflects the pattern of the Father's love to us in his living and dying; we reflect the pattern back to the Father through Christ.

So we come back to the inescapable paradox. Christ must be seen on both sides of the action. He represents the reality of God to man and of man to God.

The paradox of the God/Man

The New Testament writers, the first Christian theologians, spoke of Jesus quite naturally in both human and divine terms. They did not seek consistency. They lived with the paradox of what they had to say about Jesus because they had no alternative.

On the one hand Jesus was remembered as the son of a poor Jewish family, a craftsman, a prophet and a story teller. On the other hand they were having to speak to him as the only Son, word and image of God, whose relationship with God went back to before the start of his earthly life.

It was remembered that Jesus grew up, that he matured, told funny stories, was rude sometimes, and angry. He needed human support and affection, he refused to take authority, he refused to make judgements. At the same time they found they were speaking of him as the one who:

> Ascended into heaven
> and is seated at the right hand of the Father.
> He will come again in glory
> to judge the living and the dead,
> and his kingdom will have no end.

How do we cope with these apparent contradictions?

V
Faith in Christ Today

Christians have always found these paradoxes difficult to handle. There has always been the temptation to choose between the humanity and the divinity. For those who have resisted this temptation and tried to hold on to both sides there has been another temptation. This is to try to analyse the mystery in such a way as to make a clear cut distinction between the human and the divine in Jesus. This results in a collection of baffling theological diagrams which seem to reduce both the majesty of God and the integrity of man. But usually one side of the dilemma is favoured at the expense of the other side. Many of the first Christians tended to put Jesus rather more on the 'God-ward' side of the paradox, and to underplay his humanity.

Today, as we have already seen, there are large numbers of Christians who accept Jesus as an important figure of human history but cannot make any sense of his divinity. They put great emphasis on his moral and human qualities, his evident integrity and courage. But they lose the sense of his life as revelation and salvation. For them, inevitably, all there is of God is God the Father. The cross and resurrection does not reveal anything *new* about God. It may be seen, loosely, as a paradigm of divine love, and the resurrection as a symbol of love's capacity to endure death.

Their presentation of Jesus is often moving and sincere and illuminating. They are not wrong in what they affirm about him. But they can only maintain what they deny about him by doing a good deal of violence to the texts of the New Testament. They also run into the religious objections, and the non-religious protests, to unqualified monotheism that we took notice of in the last chapter. For in essence they remain monotheists who fail to recognize the incompleteness of their faith and its inadequacy to interpret a broken world.

There are other Christians today who would accept all this. The Jesus they preach is, they believe, the authentic Jesus of the Bible and the creeds. They put great emphasis on the Lordship of Jesus, on his victory on the cross and on his return as judge. No adherent of this type of religion would presume to doubt either the humanity or the divinity of Jesus. But in practice, the Jesus they present is one who has become assimilated to the old God of superstition. He is an all-powerful saviour. The resurrection is seen as a proof of his identity. It is a kind of vindication over his enemies. Though this kind of religion characteristically stresses the grace of God and his love for sinners, sinners are not allowed to remain sinners for long. They are to show their gratitude by giving up their wills in obedience. Yet there is no

81

recognition here of the ambiguity of obedience and its power to corrupt and distort if it is not freely chosen.

Conservative religion of this kind is unattractive to those outside it, in spite of, or perhaps because of, the passionate ferocity of those within. It is based on a kind of dishonesty and in the end proves sterile. The old God of the law and of monotheism is simply re-presented as Jesus. This God is not essentially related. He is a monarch whether he appears in his Father form or his Son form. He is also a God who cannot really suffer. His relationship with the world is a judicial contract, rather than a covenant of hope. There is no room here for a real exchange between God and man. God does not show us the joyful secret of his own being, but the clever, hard secret of his will. The relation of Jesus Christ, 'of one Being with the Father', is accepted in *theory*, but its revolutionary impact is overlooked. The atheist in us goes on revolting against monotheism, either against the triviality of it or the tyranny of it. Neither of these popular, and essentially monotheistic, views of Jesus can make sense of the creeds' insistence on our need for salvation.

Those who reject the divinity of Jesus must see him in the end only as a teacher and an example. If what is wrong with us were simply a lack of rationality this might be sufficient. But, as we have seen, our condition is more complex than that. Teachers and examples cannot change us from within. Nor can they bring hope and courage to those who can have no hope in this life.

On the other hand those who assimilate Jesus to the Father offer a kind of salvation which is somehow external to the personality. Salvation is a formal acquittal. It doesn't quite require the slow agonies of growth and change, only the submission of the will. But the will is only part of us.

The Christian gospel, in its fullness looks for healing on all levels of the human personality. It was at least in part to preserve the fullness of the Christian gospel that the creeds were written. Without them it becomes diminished. We know that the search and the striving for human wholeness goes on. Often we are frustrated and handicapped by our social or economic circumstances, by physical or mental disadvantages. Yet we can *imagine* wholeness, and protest against our sickness. We sing in our chains. And God, the great other, whose image bearing down on us is both a symbol of terrible judgement and boundless hope is still the one we can neither endure nor escape.

To theological sceptics whether inside or outside the Christian church, we must press the question of the incarnation.

'He came down from heaven;
by the power of the Holy Spirit he became
incarnate of the Virgin Mary, and was made man.'

It is actually easier to grasp the mystery of the incarnation today than it was a hundred years ago. A hundred years ago most scientists and philosophers believed that our universe was an enclosed system run on unvarying and predictable laws. It was a universe of space and time, set against the vast backdrop of God's eternity. It was natural to picture God as being outside the universe, controlling it and regulating it. For God to act inside the universe he had to intervene, to suspend his own laws. For centuries it seemed as though this was precisely what was being asserted by the doctrine of the incarnation. God was the opposite of man and man was the opposite of God, and the overcoming of that antithesis was a miracle, an event of grace beyond human understanding.

The universe which scientists present us with today is much stranger. It is not closed in, nor is the matter which composes it understood as a collection of solid entities working to unvarying rules. The universe is seen much more as a process. It is an unfolding of interconnecting and interdependent trends, full of possibilities. Matter itself is not solid. Matter is energy precariously organized, which changes and reforms in relation to everything else.

If there is a God in this kind of universe he cannot be 'outside' it, for there is no 'outside' for him to inhabit. We don't have to think of God always as the 'controller' of the universe. We can think of him as its depth and potential. Instead of thinking of him as big and powerful we should think of him sometimes as very small and subtle. In this kind of universe what is small and subtle may be far more devastating and decisive than what is big and obvious. If God is the potential of the universe, then he is capable of limitation as well as un-limitation. It is part of his possibility to become material, to break himself down into the dust of creation. He can do this, not by supernaturally violating the laws of the universe, but simply by being himself in the direction of a particular human conception and birth.

God works, in this universe of possibilities, through the Spirit. The Spirit is God's agent of change as we shall see in the next chapter. The Spirit is a natural force in this kind of universe, the grounding of things and their source of development.

Jesus' human conception is 'by the power of the Spirit'. The incarnation of God is not a 'miracle'. It is within the potential of God to become part of his creation. Nor is it a violation of human nature. Jesus Christ is, in fact, more human, more individually and personally human than we are because all human possibility springs from him and is grounded in him. In his divinity he is more human than we are. He is the pattern of our making:

> Through him all things were made.

In our age, with what we now know of the universe, it is perhaps easier than for Christians of other ages to see how God and man could flow into each other, as one being, without finally contradicting or engulfing each other.

The New Testament writers often describe Jesus as a new kind of human being. Paul writes of him as the 'Second Adam'. Human history and evolution take new direction from him. The 'new-ness' of Jesus is given expression in the doctrine of the virgin birth. The virgin birth is an interruption of the normal processes of human reproduction. Jesus, does not 'belong' to the inherited patterns of human destiny. His arrival marks a new start:

> He became incarnate of the Virgin Mary
> and was made man.

> He was conceived by the power of the Holy Spirit
> and born of the virgin Mary.

It doesn't matter, in the end, whether we read this literally or symbolically. The important thing is that we grasp Jesus as the injection into the human race of the divine life. His origin is different from ours. It is heavenly. He shares our nature which is evolved from dust. But he leads us to a different destiny. Dust is not our end but heaven, which is his beginning. The 'parabola' of the Nicene creed, the 'divine history' of the Apostles' creed is about an exchange between God and man, an exchange which alters forever both human life and the life of God. There is continuity between man and God in the deepest structures of being. God has human memories which can never be erased or forgotten. Man has divine possibilities, which manifest themselves in protest and striving and hope – his quest for salvation.

The 'injection' of God into human life is the basis of Christian hope. Though it is unique it is not an isolated event. God has been present, as we shall see in the next chapter, through his all searching, tireless Spirit, through all the processes of creation. God and man have been 'open' to each other, man to the hopes and dreams of God, God to the pain and struggles of man. But man is made for God and in the end God can withhold nothing of himself. He must know us from the inside, as one of us. We are the object of his passionate love and longing.

When Jesus completes the 'parabola' of his mission he returns to God taking our future with him. The course of the Son of God through human life is like the sun's across the sky. He goes down beneath the earth's surface, and then rises clear into the heavens, like the sun at its zenith.

> Then up to heaven I did ascend
> Where now I dwell in sure substance
> On the right hand of God, that man
> May come unto the general dance.

In the ascension of Jesus, to be with God is our human hope and destiny.

Selfish genes and new creation

The creeds assure us, in the doctrine of the ascension, that the experiment of life on earth has a divine beginning and end. The original, whose image we still dimly reflect, 'came down from heaven' and now prays for us in heaven. We are not astray in a universe without hope. Within our nature, though precariously embedded, is the possibility of the life of God. We are not *determined* by our animal ancestry or by the selfishness of our genes.

The world crisis of our time has brought many people near to despair. The human future looks bleak. The aggression and competitiveness, the curiosity and intelligence which has brought us to evolutionary dominance now threatens us with our own annihilation and that of our planet. Law is no longer strong enough to check the problem.

Christ is God's new creation, a fusion of uncreated glory and the created dust of the earth. Christ has gone down and through the deep structures of human existence. He has planted in human consciousness a longing for wholeness. Since Christ we have learnt, very slowly at first, but now, too quickly, that we *have* to learn to live from love and co-operation rather than from selfishness and aggression. We can begin to believe and hope that our biology is open to transformation. We can begin to believe and hope, even though we can't see it very clearly yet, that evolution may begin to favour those qualities of mercy which will bring us through. As time-bound beings we do not know how long we have got to try to prevent our annihilation. Nor do we know what suffering may be required of us before he 'comes again'. Nor do we know what will be destroyed in that coming and what will be transformed.

But we can look to the fact that we are God's handiwork, crafted in his image. We bear the likeness of the Son of God. At the same time we know that there is in heaven a man, a human being, at the right hand of God, one who still prays for us and hopes for us. He has already come through to what we shall become. He has left with us the potential to become what he is. We can look to him as the 'prince of peace', and try ourselves to become peacemakers.

Judgement

Salvation includes the healing of our personal wounds – and the judgement of our own flaws and distortions.

The cross of Jesus Christ brings judgement upon us. It happens as God, in Christ, is exposed to *our* judgement. We try him and find him guilty. He is wounded, betrayed and abandoned. Many people identify with the lonely sufferings of Jesus. His suffering moves people from all faiths and none, because it speaks to their experience. We have all known wounding, betrayal and abandonment. But our usual response to it is to retaliate. Whether we are aware of it or not, we do repay each other for the wounds we have suffered.

The judgement of the cross is that Jesus refuses to retaliate. He brings out our rage. There is nothing worse than someone who refuses to engage with our anger or our violence. In a so-called Christian society like ours the cross of Jesus provokes a curious embarrassment. It is embarrassing because it reminds us of our own dreadful vulnerability, our fear of being torn apart by our own contradictions, suspended in anguish between earth and heaven. We see ourselves in the figure on the cross and know that we cannot endure it. We want it over and done with. Dead and buried. That is what we hope for the dark and painful parts of ourselves. That they will drop into the darkness of forgetting.

After the cross Jesus is buried beneath the earth. There is a void of exhaustion. But then something new happens which is quite unexpected. Love returns at Easter. This is terrifying, the most terrifying thing that can happen to us. We can live with death. We can live with guilt and resentment, injury and retaliation. We *cannot* live with their removal. Their removal unmasks us. It judges us with the most severe judgement in the universe, the judgement of mercy. If love can endure all that is done to it and still not turn in revenge, if love can break under violence and rage and return whole and offering wholeness, then all our evasions and emotional games are blocked. Our righteous despair and contempt for one another begin to look rather ridiculous. Our depression about ourselves looks like childish sulks. We have to acknowledge, even if we cannot yet accept, that there is an opportunity of freedom from the treadmill of guilt and resentment.

The return of Christ in glory is a promise that true judgement will be manifest.

> He will come again with glory
> to judge the living and the dead.

What lives in us, and what is dead and buried, will be exposed to the divine glory. We will know the truth of all wrongs and blessings that have been done to us. We shall know the mercy of all wrongs and blessings that we have done to others. In the glory of this 'second coming' we shall see how the scars of suffering can be transformed. Christ in heaven at the right hand of the Father, Christ returning to earth in glory, still bears the marks of the crucifixion.

The judgement on us, as on all the living and the dead, is whether in the end we can *bear* to be loved. This judgement starts now. If we can bear the divine love then love becomes possible for us. Not only the binding love of families and friends, but the releasing love towards our enemies. Because our own unbearable pain has been borne we have the opportunity to bear some of the unbearable pain of others. The cross and the resurrection reveal not only the eternal relationship within God. They reveal the terms of our release from compulsion and the secret of our own destiny. We are to live and die for and from each other, not repaying evil with evil, but confronting and unmasking evil with the stronger power of love.

The code of the kingdom

But what about those for whom life seems to have brought only tragedy? What is salvation for those who have been betrayed by their own goodness, simplicity or innocence? The creeds show us a two-way exchange between God and mankind. God, in Jesus Christ enters the human bloodstream as a sign of our biological destiny. In the cross and resurrection he becomes a symbol of healing for our personal wounds.

But he also leaves us, and this leaving is also part of salvation:

He ascended into heaven . . .

The New Testament writers picture him rising into the sky. That image, as we have seen, reflects the Christian conviction that Jesus is now with God. He has taken our human nature and merged it with the boundless reality of God. The creeds hope no less for us, acknowledging human death as a gateway to a deeper communion on the other side of absence and isolation. Because of that hope the incurable diminishment of life suffered here become endurable.

But we require more than a means to endure. Human tragedy demands some sort of vindication. This is also part of our salvation, an unseen and future part which is written into the creeds as the promise of the return of Christ and the judgement of the living and the dead. These doctrines have a future reference as well as the present one we have looked at.

'He will come again in glory to judge the living and the dead'

To many people doctrines about the end of the world and the return of Christ are an embarrassing nonsense, a source of interest only to members of bizarre little cults and sects. Theologians point out that Jesus himself was wrong about the end of the world. He seems to have expected it to arrive much more quickly. His mistake was passed on to the early Church. But when years passed and nothing happened the belief gradually receded into unreality.

There are however Christians today who believe that Jesus will return in a personal and visible way to divide the human race into the saved and the unsaved. Sceptics often fail to recognize the depth of the cry for vindication from those who have been the victims of tragedy in this life. The reason for the flourishing of cults which stress the imminent judgement is that they speak to the sense of outrage and hurt experienced by many people. But those who simply take the Bible statements as a timetable for the end seem to be going back on all that has been revealed about the mercy and patience of God. His coming in the future is *always* a possibility, and we do not know how he will come, or how often, in the glory of judgement. When we affirm his coming again we are joining the prayer of all sufferers. We are joining the prayer at the end of the book of Revelation (almost the last words of the Bible) when Jesus Christ, the faithful witness, promises his people, 'Surely I am coming soon,' and the response is 'Amen. Come, Lord Jesus!' There is passion in that cry and longing. Neither the sceptic's dismissal nor the literalist's wooden certainty do justice to it. But we do not know the content of the answer to the prayer, only that the thing prayed for can hardly come short of the prayer itself in the fulfilment of God's purposes.

In the book of Revelation there is a strange and moving passage about the judgement. In the right hand of God is a scroll sealed with seven seals. There is no one in heaven, earth or hell who is 'worthy' to open the scroll. Even God the Father cannot open it. But in the end one is discovered, who is described as a 'slain lamb'. We can understand this if we see it as an inspired fantasy about the end of time. The sealed scroll contains the truth of history. We know the *events* of history but the deeper truth, the interpretation, has been hidden. Even God the Father cannot reveal it. The only one who can interpret the whole meaning of our life is Jesus. Jesus is the sacrificed, slain one who has come from God and traversed the whole human cycle of birth, suffering and death. He has shared the fate of the dead and risen into the glory of God.

> Sing O my love, O my love, my love, my love
> This have I done for my true love

His judgement, like his living and dying, is a judgement of mercy. He is our friend. He is on our side. His judgement is the final hope for those who have known only tragedy in this life. They will see the pattern whole. They will know their pain made fruitful.

The identity of Jesus as the Son of God, his incarnation, death, resurrection, ascension and return to judge are movements of the divine dance. Each movement redeems part of reality for the kingdom of God. The kingdom is our hope of changed values and right relationships. It is the kingdom of heaven, the solid and lasting reality into which this transient world is to be born.

We should always remember that in the Nicene version the second part of the creed enters with a declaration of faith in the unshakeable reality of the kingdom:

> And his kingdom shall have no end.

NOTES

1 From the traditional Cornish carol 'Tomorrow Shall be my Dancing Day'. Further extracts from the same carol appear on pages 66, 70, 78, 79, 85, 89 and 136.
2 This is not the place to enter into the debate about the moral and spiritual effects of genetic engineering.
3 I am indebted here to the argument in C. F. D. Moule, *The Origin of Christology*, (CUP 1977).
4 See J. Moltmann, *The Crucified God* (SCM Press 1974) for developments of this theme.

5

RHYTHM AND BLUES

We believe in the Holy Spirit
The Lord, the giver of life,
who proceeds from the Father
and the Son.
With the Father and the Son he is
worshipped and glorified.
He has spoken through the
prophets.

I believe in the Holy Spirit.

My sister death you call me
To leap and carol
I cannot say no.
I am a dancer,
to the end
and the beginning
Of all the leaping
and the carolling
I go.

SYDNEY CARTER

The crisis of now

There is a huge gap between the Christian vision of the kingdom
and our present experience of living in a frightened, contra-
dictory world. The gap is so vast that the Christian vision is
usually written off, not least by Christians themselves, as a kind
of desperate fantasy.

Realists know that we live at a time when our world is in
danger of giving itself up to death. Everywhere there is the
evidence of human despair and rage. We feel the shock waves of
our current crisis as violence and paranoia. We react to it by
becoming aimless and depressed. As the world hurtles to doom,
so, as individuals, we drift, hoping to snatch a little personal
warmth and comfort before we are snuffed out.

91

The cause of our disturbance is the eruption of our own power. We are now able to manipulate nature almost to the point of being able to create life. We have already succeeded in creating the possibility of the absolute death of our planet. The powers of life and death, God's powers, have passed into our hands, with tragic implications. We have not, on the whole, consciously sought to do evil. Our technology has developed from our increase of knowledge. Many of those who have developed our power have hoped that we would gain greater peace, equality, progress and security. Instead we have become desperately insecure and vulnerable. Our knowledge has left us isolated. We are dislocated from the past by our terrible secret. We are unable to imagine a human future that won't be worse than the present. Old people shudder when they think of the world their grandchildren will inhabit and are glad that they will be dead.

The irony is that it is precisely because we control so much of our environment that we have lost our place within it. We don't belong any more. We no longer feel that our lives are bounded by great natural forces. We are no longer sustained by the sense of a deep matrix of recreative energy. Becoming God-like, we have lost God.

In one sense this represents an intensification of the perennial human problems we considered in the last chapter. But in another sense it represents an entirely new dilemma. The pressure on individuals is of a different kind. In the past human beings have been saddened by the thought of their own deaths. Sadness about death and fear of it have driven many to search for God. It is natural to grieve at the thought that the world will go on without us, that the time will come when our eyes will no longer open to sunlight. Sadness comes from the realization of our own mortality. The world will go on without us. Irreplaceable as we are in our own eyes and in the eyes of those who love and remember us, we will be replaced.

But now we have no certainty that this is true. There is no guarantee that life will go on without us. The death of the individual has no significance at all compared to the 'megadeath' which threatens us. Sadness about our own death only makes sense if life is to go on without us. If the whole life of the planet is threatened both life and death lose their meaning. We don't know how to die because we have never had to live with this degree of insecurity. Faced with the prospect of our own personal death the temptation is either to 'get it over', by throwing our lives away, or to cling in desperation to the little we have left, hurt beyond grief by the insignificance of our departure.

Crisis and religion

Religion seems unable to solve the crisis. In the deepest sense it is a religious crisis because it has to do with the horizons and boundaries of human life. It forces back the question of whether this life does have any meaning or givenness apart from what we invent for it. There is something embarrassing about this question because it is so obvious and so painful. We laugh as television clowns and comics parody our preoccupation with the 'meaning of life'. The intensity which they mock is one we cannot admit to. It hurts so much that the only way we can deal with it is through jokes. And they are very *funny*, like the best jokes about the crucifixion. If we didn't laugh we'd cry.

Religion is not only unable to solve the crisis, it sometimes prevents the crisis from being faced. Religious people find it easy to tut and groan about the state of the world. In doing so they dissociate themselves from the problem. For the pious the world *can*, as it were, 'go to hell'. They have found peace with God.

But this won't do. Those who have faith and recognize God's agony for the world cannot escape into religious security. But if *they* try to articulate the gospel in the language of the present world, they often seem forced by the contradictions into broken and confused speech. The God they present is a weak and baffled God, as weak and baffled by our dilemmas as we are.

Most non-religious people realize that these are desperate strategies. They write off religion because it is clear that it has no power to interpret the present time. It is experienced as 'irrelevant'. Religious people, in their turn, frequently misunderstand the cry of 'irrelevance'. They think they are being asked to make political, moral or economic judgements on the present world. When they do so, because religious people are not notably wiser or better-informd than others, all that they can come up with are platitudes and clichés, which confirm the suspicion that religion has nothing to offer.

What is needed is interpretation. People need resources to cope with the present dislocation in ways which do not separate them from the rest of the human community, but weave them deeply into it as agents of hope and mercy.

The Holy Spirit

The creeds affirm belief in the Holy Spirit. The Apostles' creed does not elaborate, but makes the clause about the Spirit the beginning of its third and last section. The Nicene creed adopts a vagueness of language quite unlike the very precise language used in the section about Jesus Christ:

> We believe in the Holy Spirit,
> The Lord, the giver of life,
> who proceeds from the Father [and the Son].
> With the Father and the Son he is worshipped and glorified.
> He has spoken through the prophets.

All this is rather mysterious. It seems that the creed makers were particularly uneasy about saying too much. Human language about the Holy Spirit must remain as open and un-committed as possible.[1]

The strangeness of language about the Holy Spirit is a reflec-tion of the fact that the Spirit has a lot to do with the future. The New Testament describes the Spirit as the Spirit of the age to come. It is as though God is pointing us into the unknown. It is the unknown of his own fulfilment. We have no programme of what it contains because it is being worked out now and we are part of it.

The Holy Spirit in the New Testament

We can deduce this from the New Testament. The Spirit comes to the disciples of Jesus as a gift from God. In the Gospel of John the coming of the Spirit is promised by Jesus. The disciples do not know in advance what the gift contains. The coming of the Spirit is dependent on the departure of Jesus. The gift can, as it were, only be released by the death and departure of Jesus. The character of the Spirit is love and truth. The Spirit is to be the 'advocate', bringing deep help from God, counsel and encour-agement to the Christian community.

In the Acts of the Apostles the coming of the Spirit is a dramatic event. The disciples of Jesus are empowered to preach. They 'speak in tongues'. The Spirit is what drives the mission of Jesus on, from the cross to the kingdom, through his disciples. Again it is the cross and resurrection of Jesus which has some-how released this burst of interpretative energy. This interpreta-tion transcends all division of human speech. In the Old Testa-ment the myth of the tower of Babel describes how mankind is scattered over the face of the earth, divided by human arrogance into groups which can no longer understand each other. The Spirit begins the reversal of Babel. Everyone hears the good news in their own language. The human divisions which cannot be overcome are transcended by God's act.

Contradiction and protest

Our human experience is one of contradiction. Our individual journeys through life are flawed and untidy. We are scarred by failure and frustration. Our personal flaws seem to be reflections of deeper flaws in the constitution of reality. The crisis of our world at present has manifested in all its horror the gap between human aspiration and actual human achievement.

The cross of Jesus gives us an image of the human person totally exposed to these contradictions. The Son of Man who has brought life to others cannot come down from the cross. He is pinned, helpless, to the reality of it, naked between earth and heaven. He can do nothing to relieve or end his suffering. The cross is a symbol of universal experience. It is part of what it means to be a human person, *any* human person. In our time we can see the cross as a symbol for the whole of mankind's condition. We are crucified by our own contradictions, between power and powerlessness, strength and weakness, love and aggression, healing and destruction.

What arises from this contradiction is *protest*. We cannot believe the intensity of the pain. Our hearts refuse to accept that this is the last word of reality. Jesus, on the cross, articulated the protest as a cry to God. His abandonment by God opened him to the depths of the abyss which all creatures dread. The protest from the cross, the protest of all creatures looking into the nightmare of unresolved contradiction, would not arise if we were incapable of hope. It is because we know that it *should not be so* that our hearts cry out. It is because somewhere deep in us is a memory of something that we have not yet experienced except in our imagination. We can *imagine* the resolution of contradiction, the healing of the abyss, the dream of communion overcoming dereliction. Fairy tales and myths, soap operas and songs, insist that this *must* be part of the human story. The cry from the cross is already a cry for the coming of the Holy Spirit. In our created nature there is something that revolts, that rebels against despair. The dark beginning of the cry for the Spirit is a cry of brokenness and torment. But it is a

95

cry that, faithfully articulated, clears the darkness for the Spirit's descent.

Prophecy

The creed says that the Holy Spirit 'has spoken through the prophets'. The first Christians searched the Old Testament to find 'predictions' of the death and resurrection of Jesus. They pinpointed specific passages which seemed to them to describe ahead of time the things that Jesus had suffered. But these specific predictions, compelling and intriguing though they are, are only part of the much wider way in which 'the age to come' is anticipated in human brokenness and in the persistence of human hope. The Holy Spirit has spoken, not only through the prophets of the Old and New Testaments, but through the prophetic hopes of other religious traditions, and perhaps also through the folk wisdom of many ages and cultures. Prophets are those who speak for God. True prophets seem to come with a double-edged message. There is judgement and consolation. Prophets are critical of the times they live in. They see the tragic conflicts of their own age. They attack the powerful and the strong on behalf of the weak and the oppressed. They denounce the rulers of the present and warn of judgement to come. But in this judgement they promise also the mercy and salvation of God. God will vindicate those who have suffered. God will bring the time of conflict to an end. There will be a new beginning. The new world that God is bringing exists at the moment only as dreams. They are the dreams of justice, peace and community. These dreams are located in our *memories* and yet they reflect conditions which none of us have ever experienced. They are, in fact, the hopes and dreams of God for the human race which the Holy Spirit keeps alive.

The Holy Spirit 'has spoken through the prophets'. It is not surprising that, in Christian tradition, prayer to the Holy Spirit is usually in the form of invocation. 'Come Holy Ghost . . .', 'Come creator Spirit . . .' Even hymns about the Holy Spirit reflect this tone of beseeching: 'Come, thou Holy Paraclete . . .', 'Come down O love divine . . .' It is as though we know that there is always *more* of the Spirit to be received. There is always a future, which is unknown, of which the Spirit is the promise.

The location of this future, the promised 'age to come' is not available to us. We do not know how far it is 'inside' human history or how far it transcends it. We do not know how far it will manifest to us at the time of our individual deaths. The Bible speaks about this present age passing away. What will replace it is a new world. It is as new as the original creation, as new as the resurrection. The writer of the book of Revelation says: 'I saw a new heaven and a new earth . . .', and puts into the mouth of God the promise: 'Behold I make all things *new* . . .'

What this suggests is that the age to come will be a surprise. It will not grow naturally or easily out of our present experience. The work of the Spirit cannot be pinned down by the categories of normal human prediction or forecasting. But the presence of the Holy Spirit, in human brokenness, protest and hope, does manifest the openness of the creation to its future. Even in our tortured times the kingdom of God is struggling to be, and we can catch signs of it, hints and hopes, even among the rubble and ruin of the present. For our present age, as we all know, as it agonizes us to know, carries not only immense threat, but immense promise.

Determinism

The greatest threat to belief in the Holy Spirit is the conviction that our fate is already sealed. Many people believe that the end of our history has already been determined. Whether by the stars, or by the aggression built in to our genes, or by the immutable decree of God, or by some indeflectable catastrophe within the solar system, fatalism affects us – the judgement has already been made.

Religious people are often fatalistic. There is a certain reassurance in the belief that this present world matters very little to God and that it will be swept away at the end of history. There are many who are fascinated by the biblical predictions about the end of the world and regard them as selected details of the last act of our existence revealed ahead of time to those in the know. Those who are so privileged are, of course, the individuals selected for salvation while the rest of humanity perishes.

Non-religious people have their own forms of fatalism. The current most common one is in the widespread belief that the world is doomed. A nuclear holocaust is usually the instrument of doom, but the chemical pollution of the earth, the population explosion, and the steady drying up of the earth's resources are also contributory factors. Those who believe that the bleakest outcome of our present crisis is inevitable also tend, like the religious fatalists, to write off this world, and to berate their fellow human beings for their vanity and folly from a standpoint of weary moral superiority. Those who subscribe to these different forms of fatalism share the conviction that the present world is not open in any significant way to God's hope.

There are, however, other forms of fatalism, which are less pessimistic, though in the end they may prove to be equally misleading. There is the belief, supported by some Christians, and also by some Jews and Muslims, that the kingdom of God will emerge inevitably from human history and human progress.

There is the challenge of Marxism which is the most powerful deterministic philosophy of human progress. Marxism borrows much of its energy and vision from biblical predictions about the world to come. It foresees the collapse and disintegration of our present systems, and the reversal of the oppression of the poor. The revolt of the oppressed is historically determined and will result in a new and equal world, a social Utopia.

Opposing these optimistic forms of fatalism is a sceptical fatalism particularly characteristic of the old and tired Western world. This type of fatalism sees no possibility of deep change, and certainly does not expect any. Human effort and energy must go into the preservation of certain assured, and supposedly civilized, values. Often the Christian faith is seen as a bulwark against change. The preservation of culture based on this faith is worth any amount of defensive effort, education, propaganda, and weapons.

The open future

Belief in the Holy Spirit means that our future is still genuinely open. It is still being worked out and we are part of the working. The world may dissolve in a tragic holocaust, it may imprison itself or resolve itself into a system of humanistic communism or democratic liberalism. The age to come is not to be identified with any of these liberating or tragic events, though it remains a present possibility within all of them. What is important is that we remain open to the transformation going on within humankind. The Bible does not encourage us to expect much in the way of moral change in human nature as a result of our increase in knowledge and effort, but it does encourage us to be ready to receive the healing activity of God in our midst. How we grow into that healing act, and, in the growth, make choices for our world will largely determine the way in which the age to come is born. That God will fulfil his purpose one way or another is not in doubt. The Holy Spirit is the evidence of that. But it is up to us whether we receive God's action as wrath or glory, final judgement or final salvation.

So the fate of this world is not sealed, nor is it a matter of indifference to God. Those who are open to the Holy Spirit are responsible for keeping alive God's hopes and dreams for this world, confident that the spiritual energy they have been given has its source in the unsleeping hope of God himself. God acts in bringing about the end as he does from the beginning. He does not programme the universe but draws it by love.

So far we have related the Holy Spirit only to the outcome of the world. But the creed also describes the Spirit as 'the Lord, the giver of life'.

The life-giver

In chapter three I explored some of the ways in which the notion of God as all-powerful creator could be seen as incomplete or misleading. The Bible picture, I argued, was much more subtle. God, as 'Father', does indeed call the universe into existence. But God's calling is less of an order and more of a permission: 'Let there be Light . . .' It is a giving up of part of his freedom, an act of sacrifice. God the creator does not build a universe to extend his power but to increase joy. The Father is not all there is of God, there is eternally within God the action and passion of love and response. The universe is created as part of this love, and in the universe God is allowing the possibility of free creatures being caught up into his dance of love.

But there is a third term in this dance. The third term is the gift itself, the love of the Father for the Son. From the Father comes Spirit, and the Spirit is the transmitter of the Father's life, his being and reality. God the Father does not dominate creation. He sacrifices himself for it, withdrawing his power. But he gives himself to the creation in a way that is internal to its own structure, through the Son and the Spirit.

Because there is a universe, most of the ways in which we speak of God the Father will be in mythic, prehistoric terms. God the Father is a darkness, a void, an enigma beyond our comprehension. The Father operates in the universe through the Son and the Spirit. The Son is reflected in the universe as the image of God, the possibility of the evolution of free men and women. In time, as we have seen, the original is born into the universe as Jesus Christ to manifest our destiny. He reveals to us and releases in us the image of God.

Jesus Christ is the goal of creation. The Holy Spirit, on the other hand, is God imminent, working, hidden, through the possibilities of the universe. The Holy Spirit is God's gift of himself, not in human form, but in the form of a universal love which is capable of every and any embodiment. Through the Holy Spirit the unconscious processes of the cosmos are open to subtle divine influence. The Holy Spirit is the inescapable lure that is gently and patiently drawing the possibilities of the universe into alignment with God's hope. Jesus Christ has a two-fold nature. The Spirit is manifold (a point which is represented by the descriptions of the Spirit in Scripture and hymnody as 'sevenfold'). The origin of Jesus Christ is in God the Father. But because he is the true son in whose image all the rest of us are made he is also more truly and authentically human than the rest of us have yet become. In the same way the origin of the Holy Spirit is in God the Father. The Spirit 'proceeds' from the Father. The root meaning of Spirit, in Hebrew and Greek, is 'breath'. The Spirit is what the Father breathes into creation. Breath is invisible. It stands for life. It is what makes the creation able to evolve, change, and bring forth life of its own. The Spirit does not operate by supernatural force. Like Jesus Christ, though the Spirit's origins are elsewhere, there is an inextricable intertwining of the Spirit with the processes of the created universe. The Spirit manifests in the creative convergence and innovatory potential of natural powers. The Spirit is the divine ground of creation. The creed affirms the Spirit as:

> The Lord, the giver of life,
> who proceeds from the Father.

Creator Spirit

To speak of the Holy Spirit as the giver of life is not a specific reference to the emergence of biological life on earth. It has more to do with the idea of the Spirit as the 'breath' of God the Father, the Father's life transmitted in a hidden and self-effacing way to the evolving universe. The Holy Spirit tells us a great deal about creation.

Earlier we looked at the objections which come from atheism and Buddhism to the idea of a creator God. I argued that their objections are overwhelming if we continue to see God, as many of us have been taught to do, as a kind of cosmic engineer. Instead, I have suggested that we need to see the activity of God as a dialogue. God speaks his creative word, and is prepared to wait a long time for an answer. But what about the pain and frustration involved in that long wait?

Once we let go of superstitious notions of God our attitude to the apparent waste and frustration in the universe will begin to change. The 'inefficiency' of evolution will no longer be an argument against God. We shall realize that the purpose of God is not to find the quickest way to produce intelligent life but to extend in generosity the abundance of his joy. God the Holy Spirit brings delight to the Father by enabling and releasing the inventiveness of creation. Part of God's dance is exploring the different ways in which the creatures of the earth *can* be large or small, fast or hairy, agile or sleepy, prickly or intelligent. The Holy Spirit is shockingly wasteful of time and energy. But that is because creation is not destined for a *particular* end. It is destined for glory. Only play and struggle and experiment give time and space sufficient for glory to emerge.

Notions of 'waste' are out of place because God takes a delight in all there is, simply because it is. Whatever comes to be from the breath of God, whether it is alive or inanimate is within the orbit of the dance of God. It is to be celebrated whether it lives or dies. It is God's creation even if it turns out to be freak or a monster, or if it produces a mutation which leads to an evolutionary dead end. God does not see freaks and dead ends as failures, as we do, with our narrow, functional, tidy minds. God is not tidy.

But he is economical. There is a recognizable economy in creation, in the structure of the galaxies and in microspace, in the interlocking and interdependence of different life-forms. These patterns are not fixed. They depend on disruption and disintegration. In the natural world life feeds off life. Violence and accident, chance and collision are all part of the process. Here we come again to the problem of which Buddhists and atheists, and many others, speak. How can these negative and disruptive elements serve the cause of love? The problem can be taken at different levels.

The Spirit, death and suffering

Intellectually we can appreciate that in a universe like ours, which is designed to evolve, death is a necessity. Death and chance are the mechanisms of change. The Spirit which gives life improvises on the theme of death, making it fruitful. The necessary 'flaw' of death is one of the Spirit's tools. Through the natural world runs the pattern of life for life, death for death. Within this there are forms of life which seem to be totally destructive. Germs and viruses, injurious parasites and cancers. Our human imagination protests at the thought that God also rejoices in them.

There are other disruptions, 'acts of God', which terrify. Lightning and earthquakes have sometimes been seen as manifestations of God's splendour. We know what causes them and that they are natural phenomena. They are not in themselves to be assessed as good or evil. But when they bring ruin to human populations we have a tendency to ask, 'Why did God let it happen?'

It may disturb us to think of a hungry lion tearing a zebra apart and devouring it for its dinner. But it disturbs us far more when a lion attacks and tears to pieces a helpless child. We are bound to ask, 'How *can* there be a God?' We may acknowledge the necessity for killers and predators in the universe, but when we discover that we are fatally ill we ask, 'Why me?'

This questioning is hardly surprising. For conscious beings death is the deepest threat, for we go into it knowing and *un*knowing. When death is accompanied by violence and pain we are bound to protest. We begin to see all the other signs of disruption in the universe as evidence of the tragic flaw which seems to be woven into the creation. For human hearts there is always a superfluity of sorrow.

Yet only human beings can ask God, 'Why?' With our vulnerability goes privilege. Only man can demand an answer from God, can put him, as it were, on trial, can question and reject him. Only man can ask God, from the depth of his pain, whether the universe will have been, in the end, worthwhile.

In the book of Job, in the Old Testament, answers are demanded of God. Job rails at God for the misfortunes of his life. He refuses to accept his sufferings without a proper explanation. He rejects the conventional religious views of his friends who tell him that it is impious to question God. God, Job insists, must vindicate himself.

God does answer Job 'out of the whirlwind'. But his answer is in the form of an impossible question, 'Where were you when I laid the foundations of the earth?' That, of course, is not an answer, but we should not take it as a mere dismissal of the original question. In 'laying the foundations of the earth' God has exposed the mystery of sacrifice which is, as we have seen, part of his own nature. Sacrifice and suffering, the exchange of life for life, is at the core of the life of God. It is rooted in his will, and runs like a red line of blood through all creation. Job's sufferings have brought him to dereliction. But in his integrity, in his refusal and protest, he is actually brought face to face with God. By answering Job, even with a riddle, God becomes *present* to him.

God neither explains, nor disowns, the 'flaw' in created reality. The 'flaw' in fact reveals his own heart. Job feels that his sufferings have cut him off from God. He experiences divine silence. This is a common experience of sufferers. There is no answer or explanation from God until the darkness is wholly confronted and entered. Then the closeness of God is discovered, by his own deep presence in the darkness of loss and disintegration.

The Bible suggests that God has particular care for those who suffer. The weak, the wounded, the poor and the bereaved are his particular friends. This is not sentimentality, it is the recognition that sufferers share in the burden of God for creation. From God's point of view they are at the heart of the dance, the instruments of the Holy Spirit. The useless and fruitless mutations, the freak and the monster and the mentally defective *reveal* God. They also expose us. On the human level it is recognized in the Bible and in other faiths that the condition of our hearts is measured by our response to human need.

This is not primarily an issue of moral choice. It is not just a matter of us deciding how much we can afford to give away or building up a sense of our own worth by taking on some dreary task for others. It is more a question of recognition. God asks us, in the poor and the weak, whether we recognize the sort of God he is. God is not embarrassed at or frightened of the dark, wounded side of creation. He does not want to be patronized in his poor, but recognized, celebrated, blessed.

It is a cause of anger to God that we fail to alleviate suffering. Instead we often add to it. The handicapped and the weak often have to bear exclusion, rejection and patronizing pity. We treat them as problems to be solved – and not as burden-bearers who are to be succoured and strengthened and, where possible, relieved. Unless we see God in the face of human need we shall

103

not see him at all. Unless we honour and succour those who are weaker than us, we shall be unable to receive the mercy and compassion of God. Not all suffering can be healed. But if we enter it with open hearts it *can* be creative.

The Holy Spirit is God's gift to all who have to contemplate and embrace the darkness of suffering. The Spirit is present in protest, and in the rebirth of hope. The Spirit makes the cross fruitful.

The Holy Spirit and trust

It is particularly important for us to rediscover that at the time of our present crisis. As we have seen, one of our major problems is a breakdown of human trust. Because we can no longer be sure that the universe will restore and renew us, we are over-threatened by the fear of each other, by the fear of loss and deprivation at each others' hands. We have put our trust in our power to hold each other to ransom.

If we are to break through we need to recover trust. In the Bible Paul describes how the gift of the Holy Spirit enables us to cry, 'Abba, Father'. This is the cry of Jesus to the Father. It is a cry of trust in which we are to be included. In personal terms it is the certainty that God will bring his purpose to fulfilment. He will not withdraw his love from the planet, though it is our own action and choices which will determine how we receive the pressure of divine love, just as it is our actions and choices which will dictate the way we receive the birth of the age to come.

We are being pressed to a change of consciousness. We need, as the Gospel of John suggests, to be born again. It is only the Spirit which can bring us to birth. The images which are connected with the Spirit are non-human. Most are elemental, like fire, wind and water. There is also oil, which is a domestic commodity and a symbol of holiness. Then, lastly, the dove, the overshadowing image of peace. These images remind us of the depth of the Spirit's activity in the animal, plant and inanimate levels of creation. The Spirit is in the dance of atoms and molecules as well as in the grace of bodies and the marriage of minds.

The feminine and the Spirit

I have found it difficult, in writing about the Holy Spirit, to use the conventional masculine pronoun. I have, in fact, avoided it, at the cost of some tortuous prose. Perhaps it is because the crisis of our time requires us to become much more aware of the so-called feminine values of nurturance, patience and compassion. The source of these values is in the nature of God, for we are made, male and female, 'in his image'.

There has been a long ambivalence about the feminine in Christian tradition. Worship of the 'feminine' aspects of God has never been quite accepted or acceptable. Worship of the 'masculine' aspects has been accepted far too uncritically. One English woman mystic of the fourteeth century, Julian of Norwich, boldly spoke of God and Jesus as 'mother'. But on the whole the worship of the 'feminine' aspects of God has had little place. Instead there has been the 'veneration' of the Virgin Mary. That this veneration has really been disguised worship is now frequently recognized. Where it is recognized it provokes criticism, since the worship of a creature is a form of idolatry. The instincts behind the worship of Mary have to do with the recognition that reality 'mothers' as well as 'fathers' us.

It was Mary's vocation, above all the creatures of earth, to be filled with the Holy Spirit, overshadowed and empowered to become 'the mother of the Lord'. Mary is the earthly agent of the Holy Spirit, the earthly mother who reflects the divine mothering which sustains and brings to be each new creation. The mothering 'feminity' of the Holy Spirit is not a new idea. In Eastern Christendom great churches are built in the name of the Holy Wisdom. Holy Wisdom, Hagia Sophia, is a feminine personification of the agent of creation. She appears in the eighth chapter of book of Proverbs. The Christian theologians of the first few centuries associated this 'wisdom' character sometimes with the 'Word' of God, sometimes with the 'Spirit'. The identification with the Spirit persisted, and still exists.

The Holy Spirit, if we see 'her' as the mother of creation, reconnects us to the earth, and beyond this earth to the whole created universe which is opening up for us in our time. The Spirit also connects us to the roots of all being in the will and purpose of God the Father. The Spirit's wisdom will sustain us, if we let her, not only through this global crisis but through the heightened pressures on our indiviudal lives at this tormented time. She will bring to birth our own deep lost wisdom. The wisdom of the body, of the earth, of change and death and the shedding of blood, of birth and rebirth. She is infinitely patient, innovative and forgiving. The mistakes and flaws and collisions of creation are all to be woven, without waste or loss, into the glory which is yet to be revealed. Even the hells of the universe, the hells of our willed de-creation, can be turned by patient love into the seed beds of praise.

'With the Father and the Son he [she?] is worshipped and glorified'

The Holy Spirit, with the Father and the Son, is worshipped and glorified. The recognition that we have been swept into the orbit of God's dance compels us to worship. Joining in God's dance *is* worship, for the whole creation already moves and changes, breaks and re-forms according to the divine rhythm. In faith, we join in the worship of the stars and the seas, the depths of space, the intricate movements of atoms, the ebbing and flowing of all life forms. Our liturgy on earth joins what is offered by other beings, angels, intelligences and powers beyond our knowing.

The worship of God goes on with us or without us. To join it is to free ourselves from our narrow and constricting vision. Though we are frail and mortal it is the Spirit's work to free us to cry out our praise. Rough and aggressive, timid, grieving or angry as we may be, we are invited again and again to join the cosmic dance.

Our mother, the Holy Spirit, broods over the chaos of our inner and outer lives. Our flaws and wounds, our psychic splits and sins, our nightmares and fantasies, our illusions and self-deceptions do not disqualify us from the praise of God. Through our inner voids the glory shines out and in. For we are not only to receive the Holy Spirit, we are to become transmitters of the Spirit's life. Not by overactivity, strain or effort, but by entering the Spirit's patience and grounding ourselves in the recitation of the praise of God. Worship is our grounding in reality.

Christian worship is worship of One God, Father, Son and Holy Spirit. It is the dimensions of this divine mystery that the creeds have so far spelt out for us.

The Trinity

So before we consider the fourth and final section of the creeds we should take a look at the doctrine of the Trinity.

The idea of God as 'Trinity' – three in one – is one that many faithful Christians have scarcely begun to absorb. 'Trinity' Sunday appears in the Church's calendar almost as an after-thought, and clergy joke reassuringly with their congregations about the impossibility of preaching on such a difficult subject.

We find it difficult because, at heart, we are still very much attached to monotheism. We still *really* tend to think of God as a supreme being who might or might not happen to exist. Jesus Christ and the Holy Spirit are convenient reference points in our understanding. We might even regard them as 'manifestations' of God in human experience. But in the end, when the chips are down, what we really *mean* by God is God one and alone, God the Father. Much serious current theology reinforces this point of view.

I have tried to argue, in the earlier part of the book, that unqualified monotheism is a distortion of the Christian gospel. The good news of the gospel is that there is more to God than God the Father. The Trinity is an outworking of the conviction that God is Love.

One of the reasons why some people prefer to begin and end with God the Father is that they believe the Trinity is a divisive doctrine. They assume that a simple, uncluttered belief in one God would unite the different religions of the world. But what unites the different faiths is not a common rationally worked-out belief, but a common experience of the mystery that surrounds and envelops human life. How they articulate and celebrate that mystery differs widely.

For Christians to find common ground with men and women of other faiths they need to start from *within* the experience of mystery as it has come down to them through the Scriptures and the creeds. If they start from a rationally worked-out invention, however intellectually neat and plausible, they have no common ground with anyone.

Christianity, if it stays grounded in the Trinity, is an enormously flexible and wide-open faith. It is the Trinity that gives it common ground with the two great poles of religious experience, and enables it to learn from and contribute to, the different faiths of the world.

In search of the East pole and the West pole

We have already distinguished briefly between the kind of religions that work from the outside inwards and those that work from the inside outwards. There seem to be two poles of religious experience. They crop up in some form or another not only across the spectrum of world religions but within each religion separately. We can distinguish them, very generally, as the East pole and the West pole.

The East pole appeals to people who look within themselves for spiritual resources. They don't exactly 'pray' to anything outside their personalities. They are more aware of drawing on a wisdom and courage and peace which is at the ground of their own humanity.

The West pole appeals to people who have a strong sense of their own fragility and helplessness contrasted with the power and splendour of God. They need to call on God for help, and to express their response to him by action in the world.

The first sort of experience is more passive, the second more active. The first sort is more familiar in the religions of the East, the second in the religions of the West. It remains true, though, that both poles are found everywhere. At the extremes, however, one pole becomes so highly valued that the other almost disappears off the map. What we see again and again is that the neglected pole continues to lure those who need it even if they have to go out, as it were, through the back door in order to find it.

What this suggests is that, in the end, human beings seek a wholeness of religious experience. They need to explore the contradiction between the two poles, to know the divine both as the one who stands over against them, and as the inner depth of their own personhood. As the late Bishop John Robinson wrote, 'Truth is two-eyed.'

Here are two examples. Islam is a religion which stresses the transcendent majesty of God. The created order obeys God. It is open to his judgement and finds its fulfilment in submission to his will. God does not, in any way, explore or enter his universe. It would be a kind of blasphemy to think of God being associated so closely with the works of his hands. The Koran recognizes the immediacy of God to those who seek him – it says that he is as near to the life of man as a man's own jugular vein. But his closeness to man is seen here as a dimension of his transcendence. He is not close in the sense of being internal to the human condition.

Yet the need to express the internality of God to human life goes on, even in Islam. It has given rise to fervent schools of mysticism, some of which have come dangerously near to stepping over the boundaries of Islamic orthodoxy. Al-Hallaj, a mystic of the tenth century went so far as to identify with the divine in the words, 'I am the real'. This was to go too far, and he was crucified as a heretic. He was, in a sense, a martyr to our human drive for a wholeness of religious experience, for full salvation – on all levels of our being.

The second example is from Buddhism. Buddhism is a religion without God. In the strictest schools of Buddhism, which reflect the earliest forms of the teaching, there is no such thing as prayer. The point of Buddhist discipline is the enlightenment of the individual. Each person has to learn to understand his inner experiences by disciplining the mind in meditation. Eventually he will begin to overcome the sense of himself as a separate personality, and will realize his oneness with all reality.

Later schools of Buddhism developed new doctrines which modified the austerity of the original faith. Most significant was the development of the idea of the Bodhisattva. A bodhisattva is a being who has come close to final enlightenment. However, out of compassion for other living beings he stays on this side of enlightenment in order to help others along the way. He is like a great saint. He can be prayed to and venerated. Here, Buddhism recognizes a need in human beings to focus worship outside themselves, to call on the compassion of other beings. Again we see the striving for a wholeness of religious experience, one that recognizes our dependence on that which is not us, and our need to articulate our cry for help.

I am not suggesting that orthodox Muslims or Buddhists of the more austere schools have got it wrong. It is not necessary, or even possible, for any one individual to reconcile in himself the two poles. Some need to strike out direct for the East or West pole, and they are often the spiritual adventurers, the ones who explore new territories of the Spirit. But again, by a mysterious paradox, it is sometimes those who strike out most firmly in one particular direction who find themselves arriving unexpectedly at the *opposite* pole from the one to which they were making.

What is exciting about Christianity, grounded in the revelation of the Trinity, is its fundamental openness to both poles of experience. It is true, of course, that historically Christianity has lived most of its 'official' life in closer proximity to the West pole than the East.

The Catholic or Protestant Christianity that most of us have grown up with *is* distorted in the direction of unqualified monotheism, *has* accepted, and even contributed to, the familiar splits in our perceptions, *does* tend to undervalue the inward and contemplative side of experience. But there is no reason why this should continue to be so. In fact there has always been another side to the Christian story, an 'unofficial' or at least 'less official' side, which has shown a much greater degree of balance.

There is the ancient Celtic church with its strong mystical sense, the delight of its preachers and poets in the creation, their easy familiarity with Jesus, Mary and the saints. There are mystics like the lady Julian of Norwich with her bold use of feminine language about God and her insistence that God is not only outside us, but inside us as 'the ground of our beseeching'. There are the churches of Eastern orthodoxy. Much of their history is wound up with the history of Islam. Their members have lived both close to and far from their Muslim neighbours, sharing with them their sense of the majesty of God, but insisting also that God is community, homecoming, welcome, dance. There are Christians steeped in the wisdom of India who are trying to interpret the doctrines of the creeds in terms of the long philosophical traditions of the Hindu scriptures, the Vedas and the Upanishads; and there are Christians in China who are trying to bear witness to the divine source of 'community' in a society based on the principles of revolutionary Marxism.

At the root of their explorations is faith in God as Trinity. It is when the Trinity is lost that Christianity becomes aggressive and domineering, over-active and authoritarian.

For in the Trinity we encounter God as unresolvable mystery. His threeness does not separate him, his oneness does not restrict him. The oneness and threeness are both true. To grow into the mystery of the Trinity is to experience both freedom and security, both grounding and flexibility. The oneness and threeness are to be held together. Though they *appear* to the rational mind to contradict each other they are experienced without contradiction. The *apparent* contradiction is what liberates.

Grounded in the Trinity Christians learn to be open to other faiths. In other faiths they are seeking more of the mystery they are already living. Their witness to other faiths is not hysterical or manipulative, but low, patient and humble, based on the mutuality that comes from faith in the Triune God whose name is Love.

The eternal triangle

So the Trinity doctrine is not just a reflection of tensions within religious experience. The distinctions it points to within the being of God are real distinctions, and they arise from his nature as Love.

From the Christian perspective God *is* Love. There has never been a time when he has not been 'in' love. To begin to seek God is to begin to enter a relationship which already exists. The yearning in us for that which is not us is planted in our being in our creation. We are made in the image and after the likeness of God the Trinity.

The Trinity is where we come home to because it is where we come from. Our prayer is directed to God the Father, but it includes and articulates the prayer of the one who prays in us. This is the Holy Spirit, the 'ground of our beseeching'. Our prayer is also taken up and mediated through the prayer of the one who prays *for* us, Jesus Christ, the wounded man in the heavens.

So through us God's relationship of Love is expressed and extended. By being taken up into the Love dance of the Trinity we ourselves are brought to our freedom and salvation:

> I bind unto myself this day
> The strong name of the Trinity;
> By invocation of the same
> The three in one and one in three;
> Of whom all nature hath creation
> Eternal Father, Spirit, Word
> Praise to the God of my salvation
> Salvation is of Christ the Lord.[2]

The mysterious and ever-changing universe which has brought us into existence, which enfolds us deeper into itself in our death, is founded on an eternal triangle.

NOTES

1 From the Eastern point of view the great split between the Western and Eastern Churches was caused by the Western insistence on breaking tradition and saying too much about the Spirit. As some of the Western churches are now considering removing the offending phrase in the interests of Church unity, I have bracketed the notorious 'filioque'.

2 Traditional Irish hymn ascribed to St Patrick, 372–466.

6

DANCING LESSONS

We believe in one holy catholic
  and apostolic Church.
We acknowledge one baptism for
  the forgiveness of sins.
We look for the resurrection of the
  dead,
and the life of the world to come.

[I believe in the Holy Spirit],
the holy catholic Church,
the communion of saints,
the forgiveness of sins,
the resurrection of the body,
and the life everlasting.

Look at me, I'm   Jesus the dancing master is
Look at me, I'm   A great skill at the dance is his
Look at me, I'm   He turns to right – he turns to left
Dancing![1]   All must follow his teaching deft.[2]

Leap and carol to the Lord, I say
Show what he has done, oho
Leap and carol to the Lord, I say
And show him like the sun.

SYDNEY CARTER

At first glance this last section of the creeds looks like a bit of a
hotch-potch. The Apostles' creed lists five different things
which seem to flow from belief in the Holy Spirit. These are, the
Church, the communion of saints, the forgiveness of sins, the
resurrection of the body and the life everlasting. The Nicene
creed starts a new section with belief in the Church. It then has
baptism, which involves the forgiveness of sins, the resurrection
of the dead and the life of the world to come.

The two creeds carry different details, but they are more alike
in pattern here than almost anywhere. They are both concerned
at this point, not with God, but with response to God. They are
the choreography of our part in the 'general dance' – our movement away from the isolation and sterility of sin into communion within the Trinity.

It would be foolish to pretend that the picture of the Christian life as a long, round, evolving DANCE is an attractive picture to everyone. Some dislike dancing intensely. Being aware of a lack of co-ordination or a crippling physical shyness they dread those occasions when they are urged by the more 'extrovert' to join in some embarrassing formation: a 'Hokey-Cokey' or a Cumberland Reel. I remember the shame of finding myself in the middle of a barn dance, taking part in a figure which was too complicated for me to follow and finding myself being pushed and tugged here and there by the more able, who knew that if I got too badly out of step the whole rhythmic evolution of the dance would fail to unfold. The embarrassment was excruciating and stayed with me for months.

Still, it is the whole of life we are imagining as a dance, and we must allow for it to be a dance of such simplicity, variety and complexity that it requires the contribution of the whole creation in order to unfold in all its possibilities. It is a dance of chance, where breaks and patterns and mistakes simply become opportunities for more and more glorious configurations. On the human level we must allow for the dance to be wide and subtle enough to include solitaries and dissidents, extremists and misfits, even if their part is unconscious, hidden or deeply lonely.

The dance, above all, is an image of the unity and diversity of all things. All have space and freedom within it. All have their unique and unrepeatable pattern to tread within it. The skills of the dance are what we receive from 'Jesus, the dancing master' in our salvation; our true selves transfigured, healed and enabled for life in communion.

The split personality

In the first chapter we looked at the gap which many people experience between their public and their private selves. People who are quite sympathetic to religion, who believe in God and have some sense of his presence, often 'locate' their religious lives exclusively in their private selves. They are embarrassed at the thought of making any public commitment except perhaps at weddings and funerals when private life erupts, of necessity, into public view. But the rest of the time, to be 'publicly' religious would both expose and diminish the reality of their private experience. It would make them feel hypocritical, which is a charge they often bring against churchgoers.

This split between the public and the private is a symptom of other dislocations and inconsistencies within human experience. It is a manifestation of our unease with ourselves; our fear of exposure and yet our longing for understanding, our shame at what we know ourselves to be and yet our inner protest that there is more in us to be discovered, our relentless outer confidence which conceals persistent inner disappointment. It is almost unbearably painful to live out these contradictions. And because we can't deal with them we split ourselves in two.

There is much in present-day society which makes the split worse. We demand of ourselves conformity to the ideals of success. Society bolsters up that part of ourselves which is least truly secure and leaves us isolated in our inner being, overexposed to hurt and rejection. Our loneliness comes from the fact that most of the time we never meet another human being. We meet bits of people and respond with bits of ourselves. Because we are only partly committed we withhold trust. Our relationships with others are insubstantial, unable to endure. They are broken by a word, a slip, a failure in control. Betrayed more deeply than we dare admit, we refuse to be reconciled.

The split between the public and the private, the head and the heart, is a constant human problem. But today it is almost a necessary part of being able to function successfully in a schizoid society. To recognize the split, to suffer the pain of it, to protest at it, to hope for its healing, is to undermine the ground on which society stands.

Yet the Christian Church, in its very constitution, is a sign of that protest and hope, and the creeds are its manifesto. The creeds belong to the Church. But the Church is also part of the creeds. Commitment and belonging are inescapable parts of Christian life. And these spring from faith in God and what we know of the nature of God.

Life 'in communion'

At the end of the last chapter we explored the doctrine of God as Trinity, three persons in one. We say that our life, and the whole life of creation, rests, in the Christian view, on an 'eternal triangle' – the love that is within God himself and issues forth in a dance of salvation. Human life is created in the image of God, and our purpose is to grow into his likeness. The triangle of love is impressed in our nature and we will never be whole or happy until we recognize it.

Our journey is not that of solitary individuals to a solitary God; we travel in company to a God who *is* company. Even if we make much of the journey alone, by circumstances or temperament, we 'carry' others with us in our hearts and thoughts – just as we are 'carried' in the hearts and thoughts of others.

Christianity, then, is a *friendly* religion. Of course, to some, this is one of its deepest threats. There are those who go to church to hide from people, to 'be alone with God'. It is not the church's job to threaten such people with overt warmth. Space and lack of pressure may be the church's gift to them. The friendliness of Christianity has to do with the friendliness of God, and God is patient, knowing the wounds and griefs of individuals. He is also very patient with us. He will come to us if we cannot bear his friendliness, as distance and solemnity, as rules and disciplines, so great is his humility.

In the chapter about the Holy Spirit we considered the breakdown of trust which effects us at the present time. This issues in public rage, threat, anger and instability. The other side of this is depression and anxiety. Many people are haunted by the thought that they have become *insignificant*, that they are just numbers and units, lost in the human mass which does not recognize their individual identity.

Christianity is about the recovery of trust. The Holy Spirit gives us the confidence to remake our broken connections. This leads us to the point where we begin to be able to make commitments. We are able to take the risk of betrayal and pain because we know in the end that God is not going to betray us. We begin to become open to other people, and to give them permission to be open to us. As we do this we take serious risks. Pain and grief will threaten us, half-buried memories will rise to shame and humiliate us. We will come to see not only how much others have wounded us, but how much we have wounded others – and ourselves. It takes courage and humility to step into the dance.

In the chapter about Jesus Christ we looked at some of the problems of human power and violence, at our need for one another and our revolt from one another.

Christian life is a process of healing. We are called to dance out the truth of our being, and as we do so we come to understand our own personalities as precious gifts, needed and necessary, reflecting the bright love of God. In the action of the dance, of life-in-communion, we are to receive ourselves *back* from

God, receiving as we do so the power to give ourselves to others and to receive from them. All these are aspects of our growth into the life of the Trinity, our growth as persons.

To look at human beings as *persons* is to look at them from the standpoint of love. It is to see their potential for wholeness. New parents are thrilled at the recognition that their offspring is 'a person'. The separateness, and dependence, of a growing child are the marks of 'personhood'. A person is not the same as an individual nor is he or she merely part of a collective. A person is unique but not isolated. He or she belongs to others but is not swamped by the crowd. Our true life is one of inter-dependence.

'We believe in one holy, catholic and apostolic Church'

The role of the Church is to proclaim the three-fold God. In doing this it sets before humanity a pattern of personhood. The Church is commissioned, not just to preach this pattern, but to reflect it in its own life.

The creeds tell us that the Church is one. It is also 'holy', 'catholic' and 'apostolic' – which is a complicated way of saying that the church is not an accident. Nor is it a club, a museum, a debating society, a fund-raising organization or a self-help group.

The Church is 'holy'. It is open to, and judged by, God. It is part of his plan. It is marked by its destiny, which is in the age to come. It is 'catholic'. It is universal. It belongs to all peoples and all cultures and ages. It has the potential to become embodied in every culture and age. It does not just belong to 'Western civilization'. It is 'apostolic'. It goes back to, and is an expression of, the faith of those who witnessed the resurrection of Jesus. In the resurrection, and its interpretation through the coming of the Holy Spirit, the apostles received their commission to forward the mission of God.

The Church and failure

The credentials of the Church are impressive. Which makes even more painful and paradoxical the Church's manifest failure. It is necessary for Christians to be honest, and not defensive about, the failure of the Church. And to be honest in a way which does not blame it on one particular group ('the clergy', 'progressive theologians', 'authoritarian bishops', 'those who just sit there Sunday by Sunday', etc.), but sees the failure creatively, as evidence of the critical distance between the Church's commission and its goal.

Few can afford to deny that the role of the Church in human culture has been, and still is, extremely ambiguous. The Church is an enemy and a friend of 'progress'. The Church is a friend and an enemy of 'tradition'. The 'one' Church, which the Nicene creed proclaims does not in fact exist and probably never has in spite of the rather idealized picture at the beginning of the Acts of the Apostles. Unity is in the Church's commission and in its hope, but it is far from being visible here on earth, in spite of the pretensions of powerful parts of the Church at various times.

No one can deny that the Church has done good things. It has alleviated suffering. It has produced great saints, challenged despots, protected freedom, encouraged learning, restrained barbarism. But there is a bleaker side of the picture. The Church has created its own misery. It has encouraged fanatics, supported the ruthless, squashed human rights, repressed new knowledge and punished its dissidents with frenzied savagery.

In its history the Church is a sign of human failure. Like all creation it moves between promise and fulfilment. It is subject to the same strains and collisions and mistakes and errors that the rest of human life is subject to. The history of the Church has a tragic dimension. It cannot heal itself. When it is true to itself it recognizes the hugeness of the gap between its original commission and its actual effectiveness.

Worship

The place of recognition, the place where the Church is most truly itself, is in its worship. To some, this may seem rather odd. There are so many obviously useful and valuable things that the Church could do which would have a practical and positive effect on society, which would give the Church a 'good name' among those outside it. Worship is usually the part of the Church's life which is least understood by those outside it. And sometimes by those inside it too. But it is, in fact, the only thing that only the Church can do.

Worship is the place where the Church remembers, and rediscovers, its identity. Many people assume that individuals go to church to say their prayers. But the point of worship is not to provide a vacuum for a stream of individual requests and thanksgivings. The point of worship is recollection and celebration. Individuals come to church as persons-in-relationship. In the act of recollection Scripture is read and expounded. The praises of the triune God are sung. The mystery of death and resurrection is re-enacted in the rite of baptism or the Eucharist. Worship is when the Church relocates itself within the dance of God. Worship is also offered, not only on behalf of the persons present, but on behalf of those who are absent.

The Church articulates the worship of its own absent members. It also articulates worship on behalf of those who are *not* members. Because each person comes as a person-in-relationship, she or he comes not only with their own burden of guilt and request and thanksgiving, but with what they are loaded with from other people. Each person comes to worship carrying their own past of scars and blessings, and their own present. Those who attend worship are representatives.

In worship the Church, as a community, is exposed to God. Again and again it is invited to recognize the glory and the splendour and the majesty of God. Again and again it is exposed to its own weakness and failure and unworthiness. Again and again it confronts the mercy and compassion of God and the encouragement of the Holy Spirit. The dance of God goes on, and the Church must go on playing its part, whether it is ready or willing or able to or not. The steadfastness of the Church in worship, its willingness to recognize failure and to recommit itself to the God of new beginnings, is how it functions as a sign. Each act of worship is a celebration.

Celebrations are ways of marking human time. They are gateways. In celebration we recall the past, with pride or regret, thanksgiving or grief. We commit ourselves, in hope, to the future. We realize that, as individuals, we are part of wider events. We have our roots and hopes in times and spaces *other* than where we are now. Celebrations mark continuity *through* change. They should affirm us and give us strength.

Celebrations are also times when we play roles, change or vary the rules of social behaviour, suspend some of the barriers between different groups. So, on Christmas Day in the hospital doctors serve lunch to the patients. On Boxing Day, neighbours who haven't spoken all year grudgingly toast each other in a Christmas drink. At the office New Year party the dragon of the department wears a low-cut dress and flirts with a salesman.

Yet large sections of our society have lost the art of celebration. It has declined with religion, which is not surprising, because the ground of celebration is religious. Of course, there are always people who feel 'there's not much to celebrate' and begrudge the time and money spent on what appears to be a non-productive exercise. But most people go on trying when occasion demands, even though they are not always at ease. There's a tendency to fear the exposure of celebration. Instead of being aware of ourselves as part of a larger event we feel more isolated, apprehensive and embarrassed. We don't want to make *fools* of ourselves. Hosts and guests are nervous. No one knows how to make a speech. People spill things, giggle, or drink too much in order to 'lose their inhibitions'. Occasionally there is a true extrovert who is determined to be 'the life and soul of the party'. Or two soul-mates meet and have an intense conversation in a corner, resisting all invitations to 'join in'. Celebration cries out to us to lose our awkward individuality, to be freed from the oppressiveness of 'now' and 'here'. Yet we don't know how to respond.

Without religious grounding, celebration loses its meaning. The result is that we set limits to make it bearable. We decide to boycott the office party or to 'only stay for half an hour'. We mentally distance ourselves from a 'big do' and prefer the intimate 'family' gathering. We limit our celebrations to those we know and like: 'just the family' or 'just the two of us'. We also, without religion, have no idea how to celebrate the negative side of life. The very thought of 'celebrating' grief or death strikes us as inappropriate.

Many of the reactions I have been describing are not only 'English' but recognizably middle-class and white. Other sections of the community do not have the same inhibitions and that is usually because they have not drifted so far from their religious roots as the rest of us have.

Christian liturgy is a celebration. It is wider and deeper than the other celebrations we are accustomed to, and its transformative power is more profound. It is an essential part of our being persons in communion, of what it means, in terms of the creeds, to believe in one 'holy, catholic and apostolic church'.

Christian liturgy is a reordering of space and time. It happens in a place, at a time, regularly. But it recalls time past and makes it present. The time past is the past of Jesus, and, in particular, his dying and rising. This is the core of what is remembered and handed on. Behind the dying and rising of Christ we also recall *his* past. His roots in the faith of Israel. There are appointed readings from the Scriptures. The past is remembered, not just in a generalized or sentimentalized way, but in a specific and concrete way. This week we read this lesson and say this psalm. Next week we read that lesson and say that psalm. And we don't only recall the good bits. The intractable, bloody, obscure and boring bits are also recalled. Only in this way can all our past be made present – and open to redemption. The recollection of the past goes forward from Jesus. We remember, and make present our fellow Christians. Those who worship with us, in different places. Those who worship with us, in different times. The liturgy recalls our connectedness.

The communion of saints

The Apostles' creed makes this very clear in its clause about the communion of saints. Liturgy grounds us in the experience of the saints, in their struggles and triumphs. We worship *with* them. Through the transformations that the life and death of Jesus have brought to human life on earth, through the transformations of the Holy Spirit, the fullness of God's kingdom is anticipated. The barriers of death are suspended. In hope we are united with the Christian dead of all times and places and with the unborn.

In the liturgy we ourselves are required to play parts. We act the part of the holy people of God. In a way we know this is absurd. We remain very ordinary, very sinful and fallible, time-bound individuals. Yet God is calling us to a deeper and truer identity, one which, eventually, will not be limited by time and space. Our destiny is to rise from death, healed and whole. In liturgy we anticipate this reality. We are, in hope and faith, already risen with Christ. And we commit ourselves in hope to the kingdom which is to come, invoking it, 'Thy kingdom come'.

The parts that we play require deep honesty of us. We cannot play the part of the holy people of God if we are conscious of enmity within the community. We cannot worship with those from whom we are estranged. First the estrangement must be recognized and healed, then we will be free to worship. This also applies, of course, to our relationships with the dead. If we have wronged a dead parent or friend or lover we must seek forgiveness. If they have wronged us – we must forgive them.

As I have already suggested, the celebrations of the Church are not only for the benefit of its committed members. Because

120

we are persons in communion we bring others outside the Church into the liturgy. Our celebration has more than local or temporal significance. We are opening up the past to God, and God is opening up the past to us. We are given back memories which are still to be redeemed, and we carry with us into and from our liturgy people that we have never met or known. On their behalf we express our praise to God, our guilt and help-lessness in the face of human sin, our faith in the mercy of God and his healing strength, and our hope in what is yet to be created out of our present.

The Church – human weakness and divine power

Many of those who come to church are weak people. This should not surprise us. God, as we have seen before, has his special uses for the weak in whom he delights. Many of those who minister in the church are aware of the absurdity of their calling. Many come *in* their weakness, when they are young and frightened, or when they are old and ill and lonely. Many come because they are guilty, and in an age which does not allow for the expression and relief of guilt such people often, without realizing it, act as 'drains' for all sorts of guilt which is heaped on them by others.

The Church is always a sign of human incompleteness and divine power. It follows that the most serious problem for the Church is the loss of its sense of failure. Once the Church becomes too successful, once it becomes too rooted in the 'now' and 'here', once it becomes too attractive as a human institution, it ceases to be a sign. Once it becomes fashionable, once it becomes powerful, it becomes itself one of the agents of human oppression, rather than an agent of divine liberation. It will run its internal life according to the old rules of power. It will be-come self-righteous. It will condemn sinners and outsiders. It will become moralistic and unforgiving. It will take its institu-tional life, its services and ministry, its dogmas and edicts, its buildings and ceremonial much too seriously.

Sometimes, of course, the Church has to be at the centre. Sometimes it is forced by its memory and hope to be a visible focus of human concern and protest. But it should never forget that its only *authority* to speak and act comes from its steadfast witness to the reality of God on the fringes of things. The Church is where the great contradictions of life and death engage with one another. These contradictions are rarely recognized at the busy centre of human events. The Church has hope to offer, and prayer, and succour because it has been empowered to confront the nearness of hell in the assurance of heavenly mercy.

Baptism, hell and evil

Hell is to be outside the scope of the dance of God. Hell is to be finally, ultimately alone and without relationship. It is to be a non-person, non-human, non-real. To be in hell is not necessarily a punishment. In this life we have the dreadful power, in our wounded humanity, to consign others to hell, to put ourselves there. Many have experienced the shadows of hell in this life.

In the Gospel of Matthew Christ promises the Church that 'the gates of hell shall never prevail against it'.

Human beings are always on the edge of confrontation with hell. The triumph over hell is symbolized in the Church by its entry rite, the rite of baptism. Baptism is an exorcism, an overthrowing and casting out of evil. It is also a rite of identity. The reality of the human person is recognized, identified and welcomed.

Evil is a fact of life. It is not the same as suffering, though it can spring from suffering and, in its turn, it can create suffering. But whereas suffering is a tragic mystery which is part of creation, evil is somehow outside creation. It isn't creative disintegration, enabling new life, it is positive and malevolent decreation.

All that God has created, in the sense that he has willed its being, is good. Evil, then, must be a kind of warped being, being that is so deeply flawed that it lacks reality and substance. That does not mean it lacks effects. But they are the effects of negativity. This is difficult for the mind or imagination to grasp. Evil is not an illusion. But the power of it is the opposite of reality. It blocks and inhibits reality.

One comparison that springs to mind, though it is inadequate and incomplete, is with the 'black holes' that mathematical physicists have predicted in the universe. Black holes are caused by the collapse of a burnt out star. In this collapse all the matter of the star is forced by overwhelming gravity to contract into a single point of immense density. Scientists call this point a 'singularity'. The singularity is a kind of exit point from the known universe. Where there was once a star there is a black hole of gravitation. The force is so strong that nothing, not even light, can escape. If anything gets too near it will be sucked into the hole and will be unable to get out.

We could compare the collapsed star to an occasion of suffering within the universe. Occasionally this event, instead of making way for new formations of matter, will actually bring about the reverse of matter, the collapse into one powerful point, to which all is drawn and from which none can escape. In the same way suffering, which usually brings out a reformation of being, occasionally produces a warped and distorting centre, a point of dangerous non-reality, which possesses, by virtue of non-reality, a fascinating strength. I am not trying to draw any conclusions about black holes and what part they play in the purpose of God! I am merely trying to speculate on how evil, which is somehow deficient in reality, can have real and powerful and dangerous effects.

Evil is a kind of zero point, an exit from the universe of personal life. The question inevitably arises of how this force came into the universe. We have, for that, only a number of unsatisfactory answers. There is the myth that evil began in angelic rivalry to God. But that only sets the question further back. Why should an angel become jealous of God? The book of Genesis has the familiar myth of the fall of Adam and Eve in the garden of Eden. But, again, before the garden there was the snake, and how did he get into the garden?

Some theologians have traced the origins of evil back to the state of chaos before creation. In creating, God turned his back on the darkness of nothing. But that darkness is a kind of chaos, of what is uncreated and non-existent. Since creation it has been threatening to break in and swamp the created universe, to drown being in non-being.

In a metaphorical way this language is quite helpful. It does correspond to the way in which we experience evil. We do sense that order is somehow fragile, and that we are threatened by the possibility of chaos. When evil assails us we say things like 'my life fell apart'. It also makes sense of the fact that there is something depersonalized about willed evil. Evil diminishes and distorts personality. It uncreates because it is uncreation.

This is an insight which is often reflected in works of fantasy and science fiction. In an age which tends to equate evil with suffering, and to disbelieve in the power of willed evil to diminish and distort, it is curious how the science-fiction writers have continued to fascinate their readers by contemporary variants on the ancient theme of the battle between good and evil! The dark powers they present us with feed on personality, but they are the negation of personality. They can never possess it for themselves. The dark riders who appear and disappear in J. R. R. Tolkien's great saga *The Lord of the Rings* are faceless ones. Powerful as they are they are ultimately lacking in substance and reality.

Evil threatens us all in some degree. It plays on the inadequacy and lack of reality that we experience in our own personalities. This lack of reality is genuine. We have all to an extent been deprived and diminished and hurt by life. When we were too small or too weak to fight back we were wounded. We were robbed of our full reality. And in our turn, with ruthless, if often unconscious exactitude, we have deprived and robbed others. Sometimes we have swamped them, drowned and destroyed part of their precious selves. Sometimes we have starved them, withholding the love they craved from us.

Much of the time we have acted in ignorance. Sometimes we have known what we were doing but have felt powerless to prevent it. At other times we have known all too well what we were doing and have continued deliberately. We have all contributed to the ruthless cycle of injury and counter-injury, of attack and revenge. We have fed the evil in our imagination with fantasies, and we have contributed to the evil fantasies of others.

We can't help imagining and fantasizing. Indeed imagination is one of our great human powers and gifts. It is a place where we can work on our renewal as well as on destruction of ourselves and others. Because we are created and know that we must die, we can imagine uncreation. We can undo reality in our heads. Contributing to our powers of fantasy is memory, not only conscious memories, but memories of which we are largely unaware, from our animal past, from our human ancestors, from the womb, before we knew separation. Perhaps human evil originates here, along with its antidote, love, deep in the human psyche, and perhaps in the psyche of other created beings.

Evil is an extreme threat to us because it is not actually a part of creation. Strictly it *is* not. It does not possess created existence, which is why it manifests as namelessness and facelessness. But because of this it holds fascination for us. Because it is uncreated it has a power to rival God. We can *give* evil this power, it has none of its own. In turn, it can give us identity, the identity of our most damaged and distorted characteristics. To God, working patiently through the structures of creation, evil is something which has to be unmasked by endless patient battles. The falsity of its power is something which has to be exposed again and again. Human beings again and again have to be delivered from their fascination with evil: 'Deliver us from evil'.

In Christian theology the climax of the battle with evil is on the cross. Jesus becomes evil's victim. In his faked trial, in the abandonment of his friends, in the mockery and torture of his enemies, he was robbed of his identity, and his integrity was publicly diminished and distorted. Yet, and the different strands of the New Testament are emphatic on this point, Jesus made no attempt to argue with his accusers, to justify himself or to prove them wrong. The time for argument was over. The witty controversies with his opponents were no longer appropriate. Jesus offered no counter attack. He simply remained open to punishment, most of the time in silence. He refused to be sucked into the spiral of retaliation. He refused to give legitimacy to the law of vengeance. In his enemies he saw human nature weakened and distorted and imperilled, but he would not own the power of the evil one by calling down the judgement of God. Instead he called down the Father's compassion: 'Father, forgive them, for they do not know what they are doing.'

This extraordinary behaviour is imprinted on the different strands of memory reflected in the New Testament. The New Testament throughout is a proclamation of the resurrection, of the triumph of love over evil. It comes from the hearts of guilty men and women, Jews and Gentiles alike. At the root of it is the memory of the disciples who had abandoned Jesus and left him to his fate. His return to them, in the resurrection, was the beginning of the Christian gospel. Just as he had died, forgiving, absorbing the cruelty of his enemies, so he revisited, in forgiveness, the broken memories of his lost and exhausted friends. In the garden of tombs, in the wayside tavern, in the upper room, by the inland sea at dawn he returned to greet those who had turned away from him. The resurrection stories are the most moving, and also the most elusive, in the New Testament. We are not told what the resurrection *was* but what it meant. The lost friends of Jesus were given back their identity. One by one he *named* them, broke bread with them, undid their pain, unlocked their grief, and empowered them to recognize him as the risen one, the Father's son.

'We acknowledge one baptism for the forgiveness of sins'

Baptism is a re-enactment of the resurrection in the life of the individual. Everyone who comes to baptism, even a small baby, inherits a history of wounding and distortion. Being born into a human family is to be a child of promise *and* curse. Even when we are tiny we still have our unknown role in the battle of power within and outside our immediate environment of sustaining love. In the rite of baptism this cycle of wounding and distortion is recognized and named as original sin. The candidate is called on to recognize this for himself in acknowledging his sins of the past. He is to renounce the whole cycle of evil. He then confesses his faith, usually in the form of a creed, or summary of a creed. The baptism of water is then administered, demonstrating that evil and unreality no longer have a hold over him. He is given his identity as a person in communion. He receives his true created self as a gift from God with all its potential for glory. Baptism is 'for the forgiveness of sins'.

Forgiveness

Forgiveness is the only human virtue which is more or less unique to Christianity. It is a virtue which non-Christians find rather suspect. Indeed, Christians themselves haven't always helped by doing lip-service to the concept while avoiding the painful challenge of it. Forgiveness is suspect because it undermines the moral law. It is subversive of the normal and expected relationships between human beings.

We expect, in our relationships with each other, a fair degree of reciprocity: 'You scratch my back, I'll scratch yours.' We are prepared to overlook a certain number of faults, as long as we don't feel we are being 'taken for a ride' or 'taken for granted'. But there comes a point where the inequalities in a relationship become unbearable. That is when we break away and look elsewhere. We believe in a fair deal, in fair play and just deserts. Good behaviour merits success. Bad behaviour deserves punishment.

These assumptions are widespread. They affect not only the law-abiding and the righteous; there are similar codes of honour among thieves and villains. The person who lets down his friends ultimately stands alone and lonely. Betrayal invites our reactions: 'He brought it on himself', we say, or, 'She deserves all she gets'. Religious people see in this day-to-day sense of fair play the outworking of a universal principle. What we sow we will eventually reap. God is not mocked. Those who work injustice on earth will get their come-uppance in heaven.

In eastern religions this conviction is expressed in the idea of karma, which is a kind of moral law of cause and effect. Karma is as inexorable as gravity. Every human deed or thought produces inevitable and inescapable consequences. Our present condition in life is the result of the karma that has accrued to our deeds in the past. What we do with our present circumstances will decide our future. It is like interest on a moral investment. We are not released from karma, even at death. Indeed, death is a point of judgement, a transition between different lives. Karma creates our next life as it has created our present one. Our own choices have dictated what we are, and will dictate what we shall be. We make or break ourselves by ourselves.

Christianity does not deny that we are responsible for our actions. Nor does it deny that our actions have powerful consequences, both in this life and in whatever life there is to come. But it does proclaim that the moral law of cause and effect is not the last word in the universe. The last word in the universe, like the first word, is love. Love uses our moral laws to guide us, but will overthrow them ruthlessly in order to save us from damnation. Love, as forgiveness, is the unworking of karma, the dismantling of the chains of guilt and blame we bind round ourselves and each other.

But the cost of love is a death to convention and respectability. Forgiveness involves the end of our normal expectations. This can be extremely painful. If I am wronged and want to forgive the person who has wronged me, I must first accept the truth of my hurt. I must accept it accurately, not exaggerating it or minimising it according to what I have come to expect. I must accept the sense of having been betrayed and let down. I must try to absorb and deal with any outrageous feelings of panic or self-rejection that this causes in me. I must accept my disappointment in the other person. But I must not let this disappointment dictate my behaviour towards the other. I must watch very carefully any tendency to write the other person off, shrugging them off as if I did not care, patronizing and tolerating them under a disguise of normality. If I am angry I must be honestly and frankly angry, taking the risk of exposing my hurt. The pain of betrayal must somehow be borne in such a way that my heart is not closed in condemnation, moral superiority, or icy 'unfeeling', but open in compassion. Only if I know that I am confirming the damnation of the other in a sense of their total guilt or total refusal to accept responsibility, am I faced with the possibility of having to let them go. And this, too, is an act of love and not rejection. The basis of forgiveness is not self-righteous condescension, but an acceptance of my own moral frailty. I cannot afford not to forgive because I myself am worthy of judgement. Christian love is accurate. Its mercy and severity are one and the same.

If I find that I have done great wrong to another person I must, again, try to receive the hard truth with accuracy. I must neither ignore and evade my own responsibility, nor allow it to drown me in a sea of guilt dredged up from other experiences in my past. I must accept the hard fact that my wrong has put me in another person's debt, that they are free to forgive me or not, and that if I want to give the relationship a chance of recovery I must accept the difficulty that they may have with forgiving me. I must not try and force forgiveness from them on the cheap, nor must I try to avoid the problem by the self-justifying strategies which are so obviously and readily available.

To give and receive forgiveness is very hard. Most people, including Christians, find it almost impossible. It is the greatest challenge to all human relationships, and the only really original insight which Christianity has to offer into the conduct of human life. It is also the most creative and the most liberating possibility offered to us. It is the deepest and hardest obligation of the Christian life as persons-in-communion. It is the key to our growth into the image of God. More than once Christian teaching implies that we are responsible not only, or even primarily, for our own salvation, but for that of our neighbour's. To be persons, in the Christian sense, means that we must bear one another's burdens. We must be prepared to suffer pain for one another and to carry each other in love through times of darkness and dread. We must take on what we can of each other's violence and woundedness without allowing ourselves the relief of retaliation. Only if we are prepared to do this do we enter the privilege of the gospel, which is to heal each other and find our healing in and through each other.

To begin to do this, or even to want to do it, is the beginning of recognizing God's enormous compassion and hope for us. There is no limit to this compassion and hope. What has happened to us, and what we have done to others, is not fixed and final. The human past is open to the Spirit of God. Because the Spirit is endlessly creative and forgiving, even what seems to be 'fixed' by death still bears the possibility of change.

'We look for the resurrection of the dead'

This affirmation flies in the face of our usual assumption that death removes us from reality and, hence, from the possibility of new experiences. To be dead, we imagine, is to be 'past change'. Most of our concepts of life after death are correspondingly rather static and dull. The word 'after-life' suggests an appendix to life, a continuation of our present life in a fainter, less substantial form. This impression is encouraged by reports of the kind of 'messages' from the dead which are received by mediums, and which cause excitement in spiritualist circles. The dead frequently speak with their own voices, complain of the same aches and pains they had when they were alive, and enjoy their old recreations, their cups of tea and rounds of golf. Death has not changed them at all. They are only speaking from further away. Though this may give reassurance to loved ones left behind, most people, for that very reason, find spiritualism suspect.

The Church has usually been vehemently opposed to spiritualist practices. Its usual argument has been the weakly authoritative one that it is wrong to speculate on such matters. But perhaps underneath this is the strong instinct that spiritualist inquiry tends to minimize and trivialize the fact of death. The bereaved know death as a heart-rending absence. There is a majesty in death recognized by believer and unbeliever alike. When this sense of the majesty of death is lost, it is replaced, not with a sense of familiarity, but with a sense of outrage and absurdity. The agnostic, who cheerfully confesses his lack of interest in an 'afterlife' is also recognizing that death is not an illusion. It is a disintegration, a parting, a real end.

The last two clauses of the creed are, appropriately, concerned with these last things. They are affirmations of belief in the resurrection of the dead (resurrection of the body, in the Apostles' creed), and the life of the world to come (life everlasting).

One way of getting closer to what the creed understands by 'the resurrection of the dead' is to look at death as a natural event in the world of our experience. I suggest starting here because Christians, like spiritualists, have sometimes tended to 'over-spiritualize' death, and have lost the sense of its being part of the whole process of creation. Death, we must remember is one of the Spirit's tools.

Death is an enemy, the last enemy, according to St Paul, the 'grim reaper' of our imagination. But death is also the friend, the 'kind and gentle' death of St Francis an almost motherly figure who draws us deeper and closer into our created reality, and so to God.

In one very simple and obvious way the resurrection of the dead is an affirmation of the continual cycle of living and dying. Physically, we experience this cycle while we are still alive. The cells of our bodies are continually dying and being replaced. Nothing of us is wasted or lost. The dead cells are broken down. The waste of our living bodies has the potential to feed life elsewhere. In nature, death feeds the continuation of life. We do not drop out of the natural cycle by dying. The disintegration of the body sustains the growth of new organisms. Dead though we are, we still push up daisies. Death takes us apart and feeds us to the elements, to the fire, to earth or water. Yet the Spirit of God remains the Spirit of alchemy, and the elements of the universe are ever open to the Spirit's magic. We don't drop out of reality just by being dead. Death dismembers us. But in the dismembering life goes on. Dust to dust and ashes to ashes.

The natural mystery of life and death, dying and resurrection, is rooted in the folk wisdom of all ages. The English song 'John Barleycorn' describes the brutal cutting down of an apparently human figure, who is the personification of the process of growth. Barleycorn is chopped to pieces, dismembered, buried. Clods of earth are put on his head. He is dead and lost to human sight. But in the spring, of course, he grows up green. And no longer alone. The death of Barleycorn secures the harvest.

The Christian mystery of the cross is very close to this. The cross is a dismembering, a solitary death against the hard wood of a tree. But the cross turns out to be fruitful. Many are brought to life in the springtime of love, in the resurrection. According to St John, Jesus alluded to the fruitfulness of death in naturalistic images that are almost identical to those of John Barleycorn: 'Unless a grain of wheat fall into the earth and die, it remains alone; but if it dies, it bears much fruit.' In the Christian rite of the Eucharist, it is the body of Christ and the blood of Christ which is given for the life of the community. Life feeds off life.

For most of us, death brings with it the threat of isolation. To die is to go into the dark alone and no one can come with us. But even on the level of nature we can see that death binds us in some way even closer to our roots in creation. It folds us inexorably into the substance of the universe.

This, of course, is a long way from what Christians usually mean when they affirm belief in the 'resurrection of the dead'. But it is a start, and it is an important start, because it begins from what we know and where we are.

The creeds seem to affirm that, though death is *an* end, it is not *the* end. The fact that it is *an* end is obvious. Death is the point at which life leaves the body. The body of a person who has died is very different from the body of a person who is dying. A dead person's body is lifeless. It is also, usually, peaceful. This is rather reassuring, especially if dying has been painful or difficult. There is a resolution in the fact of death, an end of the struggle to live. The problem of disease or age or dread is over. The face of the dead person is composed, serene. The body is uninhabited. Not only has life departed, mysteriously, so has personality. The body has become a shell or a husk. Wherever the deceased is, 'he is not here'.

For the bereaved, the 'not-here-ness' of the deceased is quite obvious and factual. He has 'gone'. Death has ruptured the relationship. We no longer have access to each other. We cannot make the loved one present again because our means of presence to each other is our bodies. We can only relate to each other through our bodies. They express us. They *are* us. The uninhabited body silently witnesses the end of the relationship, at least in its present form.

But, for those left behind, the memory of the body does not die. The dead person leaves, in the memory of those who are still living, a 'pattern' of his personality. The bereaved often feel the absence of the dead as a presence. They can't quite believe that the dead are gone. They hear themselves named. They think they hear the dead person moving around the house. They forget, for a moment, the mind plays tricks. The bereaved find themselves 'searching' for the one that is lost. They sometimes feel that he is close, watching them, with them.

In the deepest relationship this 'presence in absence' never fades away. The pattern of the personality of the deceased is held in love. It may become exaggerated or distorted according to the frailty of our capacity to remember. But it never goes. The pattern of the deceased person is woven into the heart of the living. The dead become part of the life of the living in quite a different way from when they were alive.

This 'remembering' of the dead contradicts the physical reality that they have been dismembered by death. The pattern of the personality of the deceased is broken and scattered. A gravestone, a plant, a photograph, a gesture or a look from one of his children is all that is left. These reminders have no coherence in a living personality. But they do have coherence in the remembrance of love. The memory of the body, the memory of love is a protest against, and in the face of, death. It is not a denial. It recognizes what death is and *still* cries out for communion. Where there is such protest, against separation, against solitude, against present reality, the healing Spirit of God is already darkly present. In the protest lie the seeds of hope; the genesis of the world to come.

'The resurrection of the body'

Christian hope in 'the resurrection of the body and the life everlasting' starts here. It is important that the Apostles' creed mentions the body. The body is what makes us personal in this universe. Our personalities have a shape. Our hope is that resurrection is of *us*, the pattern of *us* will be reconstituted. We shall not be *just* as we were because the conditions of our new life will be different from the conditions of our present life. The model for the resurrection is, of course, Jesus. Jesus, dismembered by death, *re*membered by his friends, returns to them. He is different. At first they do not recognize him. But what they do come to recognize is the pattern of his personality. It is when Jesus *names* Mary that she realizes it is Jesus and not the gardener. It is when Jesus breaks bread with the travellers on the road to Emmaus that 'their eyes were opened and they recognized him'.

So resurrection is not merely a continuity of life in a disembodied state. It involves a radical disintegration and a re-creation. In the disintegration of death we do not drop out of reality, but through one level of reality into the possibility of a deeper communion. We continue to exist, though not consciously, within the physical fabric of creation. We exist in the memories and records of our life. We exist in the love of those who remember us. But, more than all that, the pattern of us is remembered by, and eternally present to God. God has made us for communion with himself, and the Spirit of God prophesies to our bones that we shall live. We are not beyond the reach of the Spirit's searching, healing power. Nor are we beyond the prayers and forgiveness of our friends and enemies on earth. Even if we are among those millions who are not remembered on earth, who have no memorial, we are not lost. The Church continues to pray for all souls, and, more than that, we are remembered by God, for we are the creation of his Word and Spirit. By the Word and Spirit of God we can be recreated.

The creeds do not make it clear where or when this recreation takes place. In the clause about the communion of saints in the Apostles' creed it seems to be implied that there are those who are transfigured by and through death. They have reached such a depth of communion with the threefold God in this life that they are immediately part of the company of heaven, present with us in our worship and able to encourage us on our journey. The familiar halos round the heads of the saints as they are portrayed in Christian art symbolize their transparency to the uncreated light of God.

But for the rest of us, there seems to be a gap between personal death and resurrection. At least, the link between them is not clear, and has given rise to many speculations.

Some Christians believe that at the moment of death they shall face the judgement of God – and on the basis of this they shall be transported instantly to heaven or hell. Others hold that between death and heaven there is a period of penitence and growth – a continuation of our earthly pilgrimage in another dimension.

The Bible says little about the state of the dead. There are several references to dying as 'falling asleep' and 'rest' which seem obvious enough. But there is an interesting speculation in the first epistle of Peter, which has become the biblical foundation of the doctrine of purgatory.

'He descended to the dead'

This is a reference to a tradition that, after the crucifixion, Jesus went to the place of the dead and preached to them. The place of the dead is described as 'prison'. The tradition finds a reflection in the second section of the Apostles' creed: 'He descended to the dead'. Death, here, is seen as a state of helplessness. But the fact that Christ preaches to the dead suggests that the dead are, indeed, open to change. The preaching of Christ is, of course, the gospel of the cross. The crucified one comes to proclaim to those who are fixed and imprisoned by time that the hour of liberation has come. The cross works backwards as well as forwards in time, bringing forgiveness into the past, undoing the knots of years and healing injured memories. But the dead are helpless, 'in prison'. They cannot release themselves, but must wait for the preaching of the Word of God. This makes sense of the idea that the dead are in a suspended state. They exist as scattered patterns of personality, open to God, and to the prayers of the saints and the living, but unable to live of themselves.

In the art of the Eastern churches the resurrection is often shown as Christ climbing out of the tomb, drawing Adam by the hand. Adam, the first man, stands for all mankind. He also stands for each one of us in our unfinished state, between death and the possibility of glory. In our death we are to hear the last call of love, the voice of the risen Christ, drawing us out of the prison of time into resurrection.

The creeds do not say where or when the resurrection is to take place. Nor do they make it clear how the resurrection is linked to the idea of judgement. Most of us prefer to remain vague, and we are right to be cautious, for this whole area is a playground for religious eccentrics. However, the creeds, amplified by the biblical traditions on which they depend, do provide some themes for our speculation, even if they do not satisfy us with final answers.

'The life of the world to come'

In both creeds judgement is linked to the idea of the return of Christ. Christ returns 'in glory' to rule over an endless kingdom. In the Bible these ideas are also linked with the theme of the eventual disintegration of the present world. The world as it is will pass away, and God will create a new heaven and earth. Loosely linked to these ideas is the theme of the resurrection of all the dead. This resurrection is a judgement which divides mankind, living and dead, in two. Those who survive the judgement, who are 'marked' for salvation, enter into a new life in the city of God.

These overlapping themes of the return of Christ, the kingdom, the end of the world, the resurrection, the judgement and the city of God should not be taken as a timetable of events. They are not part of history so much as the meaning of history. They tell us about the divine dimension that hovers over and in all human history, which reaches its climax 'at an hour you do not expect'.

The Bible amplifies what the creed has to say about 'the life of the world to come' in three ways. First, the world to come is something new. It stands in relation to the present universe much as the resurrection stands in relation to our present life. Like the resurrection it can only come about by the radical disintegration of the present order of things.

Second, the life of the world to come is life in a city. It is, in other words, communal life. The company of heaven is a great company. Third, the life of the world to come will manifest the life of God explicitly. He will no longer be hidden: 'The city has no need of sun or moon to shine upon it, for the glory of God is its light, and its lamp is in the Lamb.' The city is the home of the Trinity, the end and the beginning of God's dance of love. Because the life of God is freely manifest the world to come will not be subject to the assaults of evil or unreality. The book of Revelation says that in the new earth 'there will be no more sea', and we should understand 'sea' as a symbol of the dark flood of chaos which is ever-threatening to break in and overwhelm the present order of things. The pain of suffering, too, will be over. The book of Revelation is, in some ways, a vicious and judgemental work, but there is a desperate tenderness about the writer's hope that 'God will wipe away every tear from their eyes' – a hope first expressed in the prophecy of Isaiah.

The life of the world to come is God's ultimate hope for the universe. How it will get there we do not know, any more than we can guess how, in our present broken and time-bound state we shall ever be able to bear the glory of the resurrection. The future, as we have seen, is open and surprising. But the advent of the world to come is a judgement on us. It exposes us to our destiny whether we are ready for it or not.

The call to enter the kingdom, the invitation to the dance, is extended to us all, all the time. It springs from the same call of love which brought the universe into being. It is the call which drew living creatures into the struggles and ambiguities of conscious life. It is a call which is endlessly vulnerable, easily lost and distorted, but has never quite disappeared from the earth. In the great religions it has appeared as wisdom and law, sometimes as a sigh of despair against the limitations of the world, sometimes as a cry of praise to the creator of all things. It is the call which Jesus heard in the prophecies of his people and in the depth of his own being. He echoed it in stories and similes, sharp sayings and jokes. He answered it, as he alone could, by giving himself up to the tragedy of the cross and its joyful resolution. The call of love still comes to us in our individual personalities, as we wrestle with our identity. It is sharpened at moments of great decision, then forgotten or ignored for years on end. But it never quite leaves us. It pursues us to death, and, we believe, beyond the hour of our death.

But the last call comes to us with solemn finality. At the end of the ages our love does not wait. The marriage of earth and heaven is at hand. The return of Christ in glory is an image of the heavenly lover seeking the one he has longed for. 'Will you won't you will you won't you will you join the dance?'

Now the judgement is on us, whether or not we will bear the love of the Triune God. Whether we will wear our true selves, the image and likeness in which we were made. We come not to face the judgement of a court but to face the joy and sorrow and hope of our lover and maker. Will the glance of love annihilate us? Love's judgement is mercy and truth. Or will we find, to our astonishment, that we ourselves are shining and dancing in human company and with the uncreated light, healed and brought home to 'the love which moves the sun and the other stars'?

> Sing O my love, O my love, my love, my love
> This have I done for my true love.

NOTES

1 From the score of the musical *Salad Days* by Julian Slade.
2 Quoted in *Sacred and Profane Beauty: The Holy in Art* by Gerardus van der Leeuw (Holt, Rinehart and Winston 1963), p. 30.